T0144391

Confessions of a Young Man

Confessions of a Young Man

George Moore

MINT EDITIONS

Confessions of a Young Man was first published in 1888.

This edition published by Mint Editions 2021.

ISBN 9781513290997 | E-ISBN 9781513293844

Published by Mint Editions®

 MINT
EDITIONS

minteditionbooks.com

Publishing Director: Jennifer Newens
Design & Production: Rachel Lopez Metzger
Project Manager: Micaela Clark
Typesetting: Westchester Publishing Services

Contents

I

My soul, so far as I understand it, has very kindly taken colour and form from the many various modes of life that self-will and an impetuous temperament have forced me to indulge in. Therefore I may say that I am free from original qualities, defects, tastes, etc. What is mine I have acquired, or, to speak more exactly, chance bestowed, and still bestows, upon me. I came into the world apparently with a nature like a smooth sheet of wax, bearing no impress, but capable of receiving any; of being moulded into all shapes. Nor am I exaggerating when I say I think that I might equally have been a Pharaoh, an ostler, a pimp, an archbishop, and that in the fulfilment of the duties of each a certain measure of success would have been mine. I have felt the goad of many impulses, I have hunted many a trail; when one scent failed another was taken up, and pursued with the pertinacity of instinct, rather than the fervour of a reasoned conviction. Sometimes, it is true, there came moments of weariness, of despondency, but they were not enduring: a word spoken, a book read, or yielding to the attraction of environment, I was soon off in another direction, forgetful of past failures. Intricate, indeed, was the labyrinth of my desires; all lights were followed with the same ardour, all cries were eagerly responded to: they came from the right, they came from the left, from every side. But one cry was more persistent, and as the years passed I learned to follow it with increasing vigour, and my strayings grew fewer and the way wider.

I was eleven years old when I first heard and obeyed this cry, or, shall I say, echo-augury?

Scene: A great family coach, drawn by two powerful country horses, lumbers along a narrow Irish road. The ever-recurrent signs—long ranges of blue mountains, the streak of bog, the rotting cabin, the flock of plover rising from the desolate water. Inside the coach there are two children. They are smart, with new jackets and neckties; their faces are pale with sleep, and the rolling of the coach makes them feel a little sick. It is seven o'clock in the morning. Opposite the children are their parents, and they are talking of a novel the world is reading. Did Lady Audley murder her husband? Lady Audley! What a beautiful name! and she, who is a slender, pale, fairy-like woman, killed her husband. Such thoughts flash through the boy's mind; his imagination is stirred and quickened, and he begs for an explanation. The coach lumbers along, it arrives at its destination, and Lady Audley is forgotten in the delight of tearing down fruit trees and killing a cat.

But when we returned home I took the first opportunity of stealing the novel in question. I read it eagerly, passionately, vehemently. I read its successor and its successor. I read until I came to a book called *The Doctors Wife*—a lady who loved Shelley and Byron. There was magic, there was revelation in the name, and Shelley became my soul's divinity. Why did I love Shelley? Why was I not attracted to Byron? I cannot say. Shelley! Oh, that crystal name, and his poetry also crystalline. I must see it, I must know him. Escaping from the schoolroom, I ransacked the library, and at last my ardour was rewarded. The book—a small pocket edition in red boards, no doubt long out of print—opened at the "Sensitive Plant." Was I disappointed? I think I had expected to understand better; but I had no difficulty in assuming that I was satisfied and delighted. And henceforth the little volume never left my pocket, and I read the dazzling stanzas by the shores of a pale green Irish lake, comprehending little, and loving a great deal. Byron, too, was often with me, and these poets were the ripening influence of years otherwise merely nervous and boisterous.

And my poets were taken to school, because it pleased me to read "Queen Mab" and "Cain," amid the priests and ignorance of a hateful Roman Catholic college. And there my poets saved me from intellectual savagery; for I was incapable at that time of learning anything. What determined and incorrigible idleness! I used to gaze fondly on a book, holding my head between my hands, and allow my thoughts to wander far into dreams and thin imaginings. Neither Latin, nor Greek, nor French, nor History, nor English composition could I learn, unless, indeed, my curiosity or personal interest was excited,—then I made rapid strides in that branch of knowledge to which my attention was directed. A mind hitherto dark seemed suddenly to grow clear, and it remained clear and bright enough so long as passion was in me; but as it died, so the mind clouded, and recoiled to its original obtuseness. Couldn't and wouldn't were in my case curiously involved; nor have I in this respect ever been able to correct my natural temperament. I have always remained powerless to do anything unless moved by a powerful desire.

The natural end to such schooldays as mine was expulsion. I was expelled when I was sixteen, for idleness and general worthlessness. I returned to a wild country home, where I found my father engaged in training racehorses. For a nature of such intense vitality as mine, an ambition, an aspiration of some sort was necessary; and I now, as I have often done since, accepted the first ideal to hand. In this instance it was the *stable*. I was given a hunter, I rode to hounds every week, I rode gallops every morning, I read the racing calendar, stud-book, latest betting, and looked forward with enthusiasm to the day when I should be known as a successful steeplechase rider. To ride the winner of the Liverpool seemed to me a final achievement and glory; and had not accident intervened, it is very possible that I might have succeeded in carrying off, if not the meditated honour, something scarcely inferior, such as—alas! I cannot now recall the name of a race of the necessary value and importance. About this time my father was elected Member of Parliament; our home was broken up, and we went to London. But an ideal set up on its pedestal is not easily displaced, and I persevered in my love, despite the poor promises London life held out for its ultimate attainment; and surreptitiously I continued to nourish it with small bets made in a small tobacconist's. Well do I remember that shop, the oily-faced, sandy-whiskered proprietor, his betting-book, the cheap cigars along the counter, the one-eyed nondescript who leaned his evening away against the counter, and was supposed to know someone who knew Lord—'s footman, and the great man often spoken of, but rarely seen—he who made "a two-'undred pound book on the Derby"; and the constant coming and going of the cabmen—"Half an ounce of shag, sir." I was then at a military tutor's in the Euston Road; for, in answer to my father's question as to what occupation I intended to pursue, I had consented to enter the army. In my heart I knew that when it came to the point I should refuse—the idea of military discipline was very repugnant, and the possibility of an anonymous death on a battle-field could not be accepted by so self-conscious a youth, by one so full of his own personality. I said Yes to my father, because the moral courage to say No was lacking, and I put my trust in the future, as well I might, for a fair prospect of idleness lay before me, and the chance of my passing any examination was, indeed, remote.

In London I made the acquaintance of a great blonde man, who talked incessantly about beautiful women, and painted them sometimes larger than life, in somnolent attitudes, and luxurious tints. His studio was a welcome contrast to the spitting and betting of the tobacco shop. His pictures—Doré-like improvisations, devoid of skill, and, indeed, of artistic perception, save a certain sentiment for the grand and noble—

filled me with wonderment and awe. "How jolly it would be to be a painter," I once said, quite involuntarily. "Why, would you like to be a painter?" he asked abruptly. I laughed, not suspecting that I had the slightest gift, as indeed was the case, but the idea remained in my mind, and soon after I began to make sketches in the streets and theatres. My attempts were not very successful, but they encouraged me to tell my father that I would go to the military tutor no more, and he allowed me to enter the Kensington Museum as an Art student. There, of course, I learned nothing, and, from the point of view of art merely, I had much better have continued my sketches in the streets; but the museum was a beautiful and beneficent influence, and one that applied marvellously well to the besetting danger of the moment; for in the galleries I met young men who spoke of other things than betting and steeplechase riding, who, I remember, it was clear to me then, looked to a higher ideal than mine, breathed a purer atmosphere of thought than I. And then the sweet, white peace of antiquity! The great, calm gaze that is not sadness nor joy, but something that we know not of—which is lost to the world forever.

"But if you want to be a painter you must go to France—France is the only school of Art." I must again call attention to the phenomenon of echo-augury, that is to say, words heard in an unlooked-for quarter, that, without any appeal to our reason, impel belief. France! The word rang in my ears and gleamed in my eyes. France! All my senses sprang from sleep like a crew when the man on the look-out cries, "Land ahead!" Instantly I knew I should, that I must, go to France, that I would live there, that I would become as a Frenchman. I knew not when nor how, but I knew I should go to France. . .

So my youth ran into manhood, finding its way from rock to rock like a rivulet, gathering strength at each leap. One day my father was suddenly called to Ireland. A few days after, a telegram came, and my mother read that we were required at his bedside. We journeyed over land and sea, and on a bleak country road, one winter's evening, a man approached us and I heard him say that all was over, that my father was dead. I loved my father; I burst into tears; and yet my soul said, "I am glad." The thought came unbidden, undesired, and I turned aside, shocked at the sight it afforded of my soul.

O, my father, I, who love and reverence nothing else, love and reverence thee; thou art the one pure image in my mind, the one true affection that life has not broken or soiled; I remember thy voice and thy kind, happy ways. All I have of worldly goods and native wit I received from thee—and was it I who was glad? No, it was not I; I had no concern in the thought that then fell upon me unbidden and undesired; my individual voice can give you but praise and loving words; and the voice that said "I am glad" was not my voice, but that of the will to live which we inherit from elemental dust through countless generations. Terrible and imperative is the voice of the will to live: let him who is innocent cast the first stone.

Terrible is the day when each sees his soul naked, stripped of all veil; that dear soul which he cannot change or discard, and which is so irreparably his.

My father's death freed me, and I sprang like a loosened bough up to the light. His death gave me power to create myself, that is to say, to create a complete and absolute self out of the partial self which was all that the restraint of home had permitted; this future self, this ideal George Moore, beckoned me, lured like a ghost; and as I followed the funeral the question, Would I sacrifice this ghostly self, if by so doing I should bring my father back? presented itself without intermission, and I shrank horrified at the answer which I could not crush out of mind.

Now my life was like a garden in the emotive torpor of spring; now my life was like a flower conscious of the light. Money was placed in my hands, and I divined all it represented. Before me the crystal lake, the distant mountains, the swaying woods, said but one word, and that word was—self; not the self that was then mine, but the self on whose creation I was enthusiastically determined. But I felt like a murderer when I turned to leave the place which I had so suddenly, and I could not but think unjustly, become possessed of. And now, as I probe this poignant psychological moment, I find that, although I perfectly well realised that all pleasures were then in my reach—women, elegant dress, theatres, and supper-rooms, I hardly thought at all of them, and much more of certain drawings from the plaster cast. I would be an artist. More than ever I was determined to be an artist, and my brain was made of this desire as I journeyed as fast as railway and steamboat could take me to London. No further trammels, no further need of being a soldier, of being anything but myself; eighteen, with life and France before me! But the spirit did not move me yet to leave home. I would feel the pulse of life at home before I felt it abroad. I would hire a studio. A studio— tapestries, smoke, models, conversations. But here it is difficult not to convey a false impression. I fain would show my soul in these pages, like a face in a pool of clear water; and although my studio was in truth no more than an amusement, and a means of effectually throwing over all restraint, I did not view it at all in this light. My love of Art was very genuine and deep-rooted; the tobacconist's betting-book was now as nothing, and a certain Botticelli in the National Gallery held me in tether. And when I look back and consider the past, I am forced to admit that I might have grown up in less fortunate circumstances, for even the studio, with its dissipations—and they were many—was not unserviceable; it developed the natural man, who educates himself, who allows his mind to grow and ripen under the sun and wind of modern life, in contradistinction to the University man, who is fed upon the dust of ages, and after a formula which has been composed to suit the requirements of the average human being.

Nor was my reading at this time so limited as might be expected from the foregoing. The study of Shelley's poetry had led me to read very nearly all the English lyric poets; Shelley's atheism had led me to read Kant, Spinoza, Godwin, Darwin, and Mill. So it will be understood that Shelley not only gave me my first soul, but led all its first flights. But I do not think that if Shelley had been no more than a poet, notwithstanding my very genuine love of verse, he would have gained such influence in my youthful sympathies; but Shelley dreamed in metaphysics—very thin dreaming if you will; but just such thin dreaming as I could follow. Was there or was there not a God? And for many years I could not dismiss as parcel of the world's folly this question, and I sought a solution, inclining towards atheism, for it was natural in me to revere nothing, and to oppose the routine of daily thought. And I was but sixteen when I resolved to tell my mother that I must decline to believe any longer in a God. She was leaning against the chimney-piece in the drawing-room. I expected to paralyse the household with the news; but although a religious woman, my mother did not seem in the least frightened, she only said, "I am very sorry, George, it is so." I was deeply shocked at her indifference.

Finding music and atheism in poetry I cared little for novels. Scott seemed to me on a par with Burke's speeches; that is to say, too impersonal for my very personal taste. Dickens I knew by heart, and *Bleak House* I thought his greatest achievement. Thackeray left no deep impression on my mind; in no way did he hold my thoughts. He was not picturesque like Dickens, and I was at that time curiously eager for some adequate philosophy of life, and his social satire seemed very small beer indeed.

I was really young. I hungered after great truths: *Middlemarch, Adam Bede, The Rise and Influence of Rationalism, The History of Civilisation*, were momentous events in my life. But I loved life better than books, and very curiously my studies and my pleasures kept pace, stepping together like a pair of well-trained carriage horses. While I was waiting for my coach to take a party of *tarts* and *mashers* to the Derby, I would read a chapter of Kant, and I often took the book away with me in my pocket. And I cultivated with care the acquaintance of a neighbour who had taken the Globe Theatre for the purpose of producing Offenbach's operas. Bouquets, stalls, rings, delighted me. I was not dissipated, but I loved the abnormal. I loved to spend on scent and toilette knick-knacks as much as would keep a poor man's family in affluence for ten months; and I smiled at the fashionable sunlight in the Park, the dusty cavalcades; and I loved to shock my friends by bowing to those whom I should not bow to. Above all, the life of the theatres—that life of raw gaslight, whitewashed walls, of light, doggerel verse, slangy polkas and waltzes—interested me beyond legitimate measure, so curious and unreal did it seem. I lived at home, but dined daily at a fashionable restaurant: at half-past eight I was at the theatre. Nodding familiarly to the doorkeeper, I passed up the long passage to the stage. Afterwards supper. Cremorne and the Argyle Rooms were my favourite haunts. My mother suffered, and expected ruin, for I took no trouble to conceal anything; I boasted of dissipations. But there was no need to fear; for I was naturally endowed with a very clear sense of self-preservation; I neither betted nor drank, nor contracted debts, nor a secret marriage; from a worldly point of view, I was a model young man indeed; and when I returned home about four in the morning, I watched the pale moon setting, and repeating some verses of Shelley, I thought how I should go to Paris when I was of age, and study painting.

II

A t last the day came, and with several trunks and boxes full of clothes, books, and pictures, I started, accompanied by an English valet, for Paris and Art.

We all know the great grey and melancholy Gare du Nord at half-past six in the morning; and the miserable carriages, and the tall, haggard city. Pale, sloppy, yellow houses; an oppressive absence of colour; a peculiar bleakness in the streets. The *ménagère* hurries down the asphalte to market; a dreadful *garçon de café*, with a napkin tied round his throat, moves about some chairs, so decrepit and so solitary that it seems impossible to imagine a human being sitting there. Where are the Boulevards? where are the Champs Elysées? I asked myself; and feeling bound to apologise for the appearance of the city, I explained to my valet that we were passing through some by-streets, and returned to the study of a French vocabulary. Nevertheless, when the time came to formulate a demand for rooms, hot water, and a fire, I broke down, and the proprietress of the hotel, who spoke English, had to be sent for.

My plans, so far as I had any, were to enter the Beaux Arts—Cabanel's studio for preference; for I had then an intense and profound admiration for that painter's work. I did not think much of the application I was told I should have to make at the Embassy; my thoughts were fixed on the master, and my one desire was to see him. To see him was easy, to speak to him was another matter, and I had to wait three weeks until I could hold a conversation in French. How I achieved this feat I cannot say. I never opened a book, I know, nor is it agreeable to think what my language must have been like—like nothing ever heard under God's sky before, probably. It was, however, sufficient to waste a good hour of the painter's time. I told him of my artistic sympathies, what pictures I had seen of his in London, and how much pleased I was with those then in his studio. He went through the ordeal without flinching. He said he would be glad to have me as a pupil. . .

But life in the Beaux Arts is rough, coarse, and rowdy. The model sits only three times a week: the other days we worked from the plaster cast; and to be there by seven o'clock in the morning required so painful an effort of will, that I glanced in terror down the dim and grey perspective of early risings that awaited me; then, demoralised by the lassitude of Sunday, I told my valet on Monday morning to leave the room, that I would return to the Beaux Arts no more. I felt humiliated at my own weakness, for much hope had been centred in that academy; and I knew no other. Day after day I walked up and down the Boulevards, studying the photographs of the *salon* pictures, thinking of what my next move should be. I had never forgotten my father showing me, one day when he was shaving, three photographs from pictures. They were by an artist called Sevres. My father liked the slenderer figure, but I liked the corpulent—the Venus standing at the corner of a wood, pouring wine into a goblet, while Cupid, from behind her satin-enveloped knees, drew his bow and shot the doves that flew from glistening poplar trees. The beauty of this woman, and what her beauty must be in the life of the painter, had inspired many a reverie, and I had concluded—this conclusion being of all others most sympathetic to me—that she was his very beautiful mistress, that they lived in a picturesque pavilion in the midst of a shady garden full of birds and tall flowers. I had often imagined her walking there at mid-day, dressed in white muslin with wide sleeves open to the elbow, scattering grain from a silver plate to the proud pigeons that strutted about her slippered feet and fluttered to her dove-like hand. I had dreamed of seeing that woman as I rode racehorses on wild Irish plains, of being loved by her; in London I had dreamed of becoming Sevres's pupil.

What coming and going, what inquiries, what difficulties arose! At last I was advised to go to the Exposition aux Champs Elysée and seek his address in the catalogue. I did so, and while the *concierge* copied out the address for me, I chased his tame magpie that hopped about one of the angles of the great building. The reader smiles. I was a childish boy of one-and-twenty who knew nothing, and to whom the world was astonishingly new. Doubtless before my soul was given to me it had been plunged deep in Lethe, and so an almost virgin man I stood in front of a virgin world.

Engin is not far from Paris, and the French country seemed to me like a fairy-book. Tall green poplars and green river banks, and a little lake reflecting the foliage and the stems of sapling oak and pine, just as in the pictures. The driver pointed with his whip, and I saw a high garden wall shadowed with young trees, and a tall loose iron gate. As I walked up the gravel path I looked for the beautiful mistress, who, dressed in muslin, with sleeves open at the elbow, should feed pigeons from a silver plate of Venus and the does. M. Sevres caught me looking at it; and hoping his mistress might appear I prolonged the conversation till a tardy sense of the value of his time forced me to bring it to a close; and as I passed down the green garden with him I scanned hopefully every nook, fancying I should see her reading, and that she would raise her eyes as I passed.

Looking back through the years it seems to me that I did catch sight of a white dress behind a trellis. But that dress might have been his daughter's, even his wife's. I only know that I did not discover M. Sevres's mistress that day nor any other day. I never saw him again. Now the earth is over him, as Rossetti would say, and all the reveries that the photographs had inspired resulted in nothing, mere childish sensualities.

I returned to Engin with my taciturn valet; but he showed no enthusiasm on the subject of Engin. I saw he was sighing after beef, beer and a wife, and was but little disposed to settle in this French suburb. We were both very much alone in Paris. In the evenings I allowed him to smoke his clay in my room, and in an astounding brogue he counselled me to return to my mother. But I would not listen, and one day on the Boulevards I was stricken with the art of Jules Lefebvre. True it is that I saw it was wanting in that tender grace which I am forced to admit even now, saturated though I now am with the æsthetics of different schools, is inherent in Cabanel's work; but at the time I am writing of my nature was too young and mobile to resist the conventional attractiveness of nude figures, indolent attitudes, long hair, slender hips and hands, and I accepted Jules Lefebvre wholly and unconditionally. He hesitated, however, when I asked to be taken as a private pupil, but he wrote out the address of a studio where he gave instruction every Tuesday morning. This was even more to my taste, for I had an instinctive liking for Frenchmen, and was anxious to see as much of them as possible.

The studio was perched high up in the Passage des Panoramas. There I found M. Julien, a typical meridional—the large stomach, the dark eyes, crafty and watchful; the seductively mendacious manner, the sensual mind. We made friends at once—he consciously making use of me, I unconsciously making use of him. To him my forty francs, a month's subscription, were a godsend, nor were my invitations to dinner and to the theatre to be disdained. I was curious, odd, quaint. To be sure, it was a little tiresome to have to put up with a talkative person, whose knowledge of the French language had been acquired in three months, but the dinners were good. No doubt Julien reasoned so; I did not reason at all. I felt this crafty, clever man of the world was necessary to me. I had never met such a man before, and all my curiosity was awake. He spoke of art and literature, of the world and the flesh; he told me of the books he had read, he narrated thrilling incidents in his own life; and the moral reflections with which he sprinkled his conversation I thought very striking. Like every young man of twenty, I was on the look-out for something to set up that would do duty for an ideal. The world was to me, at this time, what a toy-shop had been fifteen years before: everything was spick and span, and every illusion was set out straight and smart in new paint and gilding. But Julien kept me at a distance, and the rare occasions when he favoured me with his society only served to prepare my mind for the friendship which awaited me, and which was destined to absorb some years of my life.

In the studio there were some eighteen or twenty young men, and among these there were some four or five from whom I could learn; there were also some eight or nine young English girls. We sat round in a circle and drew from the model. And this reversal of all the world's opinions and prejudices was to me singularly delightful; I loved the sense of unreality that the exceptional nature of our life in this studio conveyed. Besides, the women themselves were young and interesting, and were, therefore, one of the charms of the place, giving, as they did, that sense of sex which is so subtle a mental pleasure, and which is, in its outward aspect, so interesting to the eye—the gowns, the hair lifted, showing the neck; the earrings, the sleeves open at the elbow. Though all this was very dear to me I did not fall in love: but he who escapes a woman's dominion generally comes under the sway of some friend who ever exerts a strange attractiveness, and fosters a sort of dependency that is not healthful or valid: and although I look back with undiminished delight on the friendship I contracted about this time—a friendship which permeated and added to my life—I am nevertheless forced to recognise that, however suitable it may have been in my special case, in the majority of instances it would have proved but a shipwrecking reef, on which a young man's life would have gone to pieces. What saved me was the intensity of my passion for Art, and a moral revolt against any action that I thought could or would definitely compromise me in that direction. I was willing to stray a little from my path, but never further than a single step, which I could retrace when I pleased. One day I raised my eyes, and saw there was a new-comer in the studio; and, to my surprise, for he was fashionably dressed, and my experience had not led me to believe in the marriage of genius and well-cut clothes, he was painting very well indeed. His shoulders were beautiful and broad; a long neck, a tiny head, a narrow, thin face, and large eyes, full of intelligence and fascination. And although he could not have been working more than an hour, he had already sketched in his figure, with all the surroundings—screens, lamps, stoves, etc. I was deeply interested. I asked the young lady next me if she knew who he was. She could give me no information. But at four o'clock there was a general exodus from the studio, and we adjourned to a neighbouring *café* to drink beer. The way led through a narrow passage, and as we stooped under an archway, the young man (Marshall was his name) spoke to me in English. Yes, we had met before; we had exchanged a few words in So-and-So's studio—the great blonde man, whose Doré-like improvisations had awakened aspiration in me.

The usual reflections on the chances of life were of course made, and then followed the inevitable "Will you dine with me tonight?" Marshall thought the following day would suit him better, but I was very pressing. He offered to meet me at my hotel; or would I come with him to his rooms, and he would show me some pictures—some trifles he had brought up from the country? Nothing would please me better. We got into a cab. Then every moment revealed new qualities, new superiorities, in my new-found friend. Not only was he tall, strong, handsome, and beautifully dressed, infinitely better dressed than myself, but he could talk French like a native. It was only natural that he should, for he was born in Brussels and had lived there all his life, but the accident of birth rather stimulated than calmed my erubescent admiration. He spoke of, and he was clearly on familiar terms with, the fashionable restaurants and actresses; he stopped at a hairdresser's to have his hair curled. All this was very exciting, and a little bewildering. I was on the tiptoe of expectation to see his apartments; and, not to be utterly outdone, I alluded to my valet.

His apartments were not so grand as I expected; but when he explained that he had just spent ten thousand pounds in two years, and was now living on six or seven hundred francs a month, which his mother would allow him until he had painted and had sold a certain series of pictures, which he contemplated beginning at once, my admiration increased to wonder, and I examined with awe the great fireplace which had been constructed at his orders, and admired the iron pot which hung by a chain above an artificial bivouac fire. This detail will suggest the rest of the studio—the Turkey carpet, the brass harem lamps, the Japanese screen, the pieces of drapery, the oak chairs covered with red Utrecht velvet, the oak wardrobe that had been picked up somewhere,—a ridiculous bargain, and the inevitable bed with spiral columns. There were vases filled with foreign grasses, and palms stood in the corners of the rooms. Marshall pulled out a few pictures; but he paid very little heed to my compliments; and sitting down at the piano, with a great deal of splashing and dashing about the keys, he rattled off a waltz.

"What waltz is that?" I asked.

"Oh, nothing; something I composed the other evening. I had a fit of the blues, and didn't go out. What do you think of it?"

"I think it beautiful; did you really compose that the other evening?"

At this moment a knock was heard at the door, and an English girl entered. Marshall introduced me. With looks that see nothing, and words that mean nothing, an amorous woman receives the man she finds with her sweetheart. But it subsequently transpired that Alice had an appointment, that she was dining out. She would, however, call in the morning and give him a sitting for the portrait he was painting of her.

I had hitherto worked very regularly and attentively at the studio, but now Marshall's society was an attraction I could not resist. For the sake of his talent, which I religiously believed in, I regretted he was so idle; but his dissipation was winning, and his delight was thorough, and his gay, dashing manner made me feel happy, and his experience opened to me new avenues for enjoyment and knowledge of life. On my arrival in Paris I had visited, in the company of my taciturn valet, the Mabille and the Valentino, and I had dined at the Maison d'Or by myself; but now I was taken to strange students' *cafés*, where dinners were paid for in pictures; to a mysterious place, where a *table d'hôte* was held under a tent in a back garden; and afterwards we went in great crowds to *Bullier*, the *Château Rouge*, or the *Elysée Montmartre*. The clangour of the band, the unreal greenness of the foliage, the thronging of the dancers, and the chattering of women—we only knew their Christian names. And then the returning in open carriages rolling through the white dust beneath the immense heavy dome of the summer night, when the dusky darkness of the street is chequered by a passing glimpse of light skirt or flying feather, and the moon looms like a magic lantern out of the sky.

Now we seemed to live in fiacres and restaurants, and the afternoons were filled with febrile impressions. Marshall had a friend in this street, and another in that. It was only necessary for him to cry "Stop" to the coachman, and to run up two or three flights of stairs. . .

"*Madame—, est-elle chez elle?*"

"*Oui, Monsieur; si Monsieur veut se donner la peine d'entrer.*" And we were shown into a handsomely-furnished apartment. A lady would enter hurriedly, and an animated discussion was begun. I did not know French sufficiently well to follow the conversation, but I remember it always commenced *mon cher ami*, and was plentifully sprinkled with the phrase *vous avez tort*. The ladies themselves had only just returned from Constantinople or Japan, and they were generally involved in mysterious lawsuits, or were busily engaged in prosecuting claims for several millions of francs against different foreign governments.

And just as I had watched the chorus girls and mummers, three years ago, at the Globe Theatre, now, excited by a nervous curiosity, I watched this world of Parisian adventurers and lights-o'-love. And this craving for observation of manners, this instinct for the rapid notation of gestures and words that epitomise a state of feeling, of attitudes that mirror forth the soul, declared itself a main passion; and it grew and strengthened, to the detriment of the other Art still so dear to me. With the patience of a cat before a mouse-hole, I watched and listened, picking one characteristic phrase out of hours of vain chatter, interested and amused by an angry or loving glance. Like the midges that fret the surface of a shadowy stream, these men and women seemed to me; and though I laughed, danced, and made merry with them, I was not of them. But with Marshall it was different: they were my amusement, they were his necessary pleasure. And I knew of this distinction that made twain our lives; and I reflected deeply upon it. Why could I not live without an ever-present and acute consciousness of life? Why could I not love, forgetful of the harsh ticking of the clock in the perfumed silence of the chamber?

And so my friend became to me a study, a subject for dissection. The general attitude of his mind and its various turns, all the apparent contradictions, and how they could be explained, classified, and reduced to one primary law, were to me a constant source of thought. Our confidences knew no reserve. I say our confidences, because to obtain confidences it is often necessary to confide. All we saw, heard, read or felt was the subject of mutual confidences: the transitory emotion that a flush of colour and a bit of perspective awakens, the blue tints that the summer sunset lends to a white dress, or the eternal verities, death and love. But, although I tested every fibre of thought and analysed every motive, I was very sincere in my friendship and very loyal in my admiration. Nor did my admiration wane when I discovered that Marshall was shallow in his appreciations, superficial in his judgments, that his talents did not pierce below the surface; *il avait si grand air*, there was fascination in his very bearing, in his large, soft, colourful eyes, and a go and dash in his dissipations that carried you away.

To anyone observing us at this time it would have seemed that I was but a hanger-on, and a feeble imitator of Marshall. I took him to my tailor's, and he advised me on the cut of my coats; he showed me how to arrange my rooms, and I strove to copy his manner of speech and his general bearing; and yet I knew very well indeed that mine was a rarer and more original nature. I was willing to learn, that was all. There was much that Marshall could teach me, and I used him without shame, without stint. I used him as I have used all those with whom I have been brought into close contact. Search my memory as I will, I cannot recall a case of man or woman who ever occupied any considerable part of my thoughts without contributing largely towards my moral or physical welfare. In other words, and in very colloquial language, I never had useless friends hanging about me. From this crude statement of a signal fact, the thoughtless reader will at once judge me rapacious, egoistical, false, fawning, mendacious. Well, I may be all this and more, but not because all who have known me have rendered me eminent services. I can say that no one ever formed relationships in life with less design than myself. Never have I given a thought to the advantage that might accrue from being on terms of friendship with this man and avoiding that one. "Then how do you explain," cries the angry reader, "that you have never had a friend by whom you did not profit? You must have had very few friends." On the contrary, I have had many friends, and of all sorts and kinds—men and women: and, I repeat, none took part in my life who did not contribute something towards my well-being. It must, of course, be understood that I make no distinction between mental and material help; and in my case the one has at all times been adjuvant to the other. "Pooh, pooh!" again exclaims the reader; "I for one will not believe that chance has only sent across your way the people who were required to assist you." Chance! dear reader, is there such a thing as chance? Do you believe in chance? Do you attach any precise meaning to the word? Do you employ it at haphazard, allowing it to mean what it may? Chance! What a field for psychical investigation is at once opened up; how we may tear to shreds our past lives in search of—what? Of the Chance that made us. I think, reader, I can throw some light on the general question, by replying to your taunt: Chance, or the conditions of life under which we live, sent, of course, thousands of creatures across my way who were powerless to benefit me; but then an instinct of which I knew nothing, of which I was not even conscious, withdrew me from them, and I was attracted to others. Have you not seen a horse suddenly leave a corner of a field to seek pasturage further away?

Never could I interest myself in a book if it were not the exact diet my mind required at the time, or in the very immediate future. The mind asked, received, and digested. So much was assimilated, so much expelled; then, after a season, similar demands were made, the same processes were repeated out of sight, below consciousness, as is the case in a well-ordered stomach. Shelley, who fired my youth with passion, and purified and upbore it for so long, is now to me as nothing: not a dead or faded thing, but a thing out of which I personally have drawn all the sustenance I can draw from him; and, therefore, it (that part which I did not absorb) concerns me no more. And the same with Gautier. Mdlle. de Maupin, that godhead of flowing line, that desire not "of the moth for the star," but for such perfection of arm and thigh as leaves passion breathless and fain of tears, is now, if I take up the book and read, weary and ragged as a spider's web, that has hung the winter through in the dusty, forgotten corner of a forgotten room. My old rapture and my youth's delight I can regain only when I think of that part of Gautier which is now incarnate in me.

As I picked up books, so I picked up my friends. I read friends and books with the same passion, with the same avidity; and as I discarded my books when I had assimilated as much of them as my system required, so I discarded my friends when they ceased to be of use to me. I employ the word "use" in its fullest, not in its limited and twenty-shilling sense. This parallel of the intellect to the blind unconsciousness of the lower organs will strike some as a violation of man's best beliefs, and as saying very little for the particular intellect that can be so reduced. But I am not sure these people are right. I am inclined to think that as you ascend the scale of thought to the great minds, these unaccountable impulses, mysterious resolutions, sudden, but certain knowings, falling whence or how it is impossible to say, but falling somehow into the brain, instead of growing rarer, become more and more frequent; indeed, I think that if the really great man were to confess to the working of his mind, we should see him constantly besieged by inspirations. . . inspirations! Ah! how human thought only turns in a circle, and how, when we think we are on the verge of a new thought, we slip into the enunciation of some time-worn truth. But I say again, let general principles be waived; it will suffice for the interest of these pages if it be understood that brain instincts have always been, and still are, the initial and the determining powers of my being.

III

B ut the studio, where I had been working for the last three or four months so diligently, became wearisome to me, and for two reasons. First, because it deprived me of many hours of Marshall's company. Secondly—and the second reason was the graver—because I was beginning to regard the delineation of a nymph, or youth bathing, etc., as a very narrow channel to carry off the strong, full tide of a man's thought. For now thoughts of love and death, and the hopelessness of life, were in active fermentation within me and sought for utterance with a strange persistency of appeal. I yearned merely to give direct expression to my pain. Life was then in its springtide; every thought was new to me, and it would have seemed a pity to disguise even the simplest emotion in any garment when it was so beautiful in its Eden-like nakedness. The creatures whom I met in the ways and byeways of Parisian life, whose gestures and attitudes I devoured with my eyes, and whose souls I hungered to know, awoke in me a tense, irresponsible curiosity, but that was all,—I despised, I hated them, thought them contemptible, and to select them as subjects of artistic treatment, could not then, might never, have occurred to me, had the suggestion to do so not come direct to me from the outside.

At the time of which I am writing I lived in an old-fashioned hotel on the Boulevard, which an enterprising Belgian had lately bought and was endeavouring to modernise; an old-fashioned hotel, that still clung to its ancient character in the presence of half a dozen old people, who, for antediluvian reasons, continue to dine on certain well-specified days at the *table d'hôte*. Fifteen years have passed away, and these old people, no doubt, have joined their ancestors; but I can see them still sitting in that *salle à manger*, the *buffets en vieux chéne,* the opulent candelabra *en style d'empire*, the waiter lighting the gas in the pale Parisian evening. That white-haired man, that tall, thin, hatchet-faced American, has dined at this *table d'hôte* for the last thirty years—he is talkative, vain, foolish, and authoritative. The clean, neatly-dressed old gentleman who sits by him, looking so much like a French gentleman, has spent a great part of his life in Spain. With that piece of news, and its subsequent developments, your acquaintance with him begins and ends; the eyes, the fan, the mantilla, how it began, how it was broken off, and how it began again. Opposite sits another French gentleman, with beard and bristly hair. He spent twenty years of his life in India, and he talks of his son who has been out there for the last ten, and who has just returned home. There is the Italian comtesse of sixty summers, who dresses like a girl of sixteen and smokes a cigar after dinner,—if there are not too many strangers in the room. A stranger she calls anyone whom she has not seen at least once before. The little fat, neckless man, with the great bald head, fringed below the ears with hair, is M. Duval. He is a dramatic author, the author of a hundred and sixty plays. He does not intrude himself on your notice, but when you speak to him on literary matters he fixes a pair of tiny, sloe-like eyes on you, and talks affably of his collaborateurs.

I was soon deeply interested in M. Duval, and I invited him to come to the *café* after dinner. I paid for his coffee and liqueurs, I offered him a choice cigar. He did not smoke; I did. It was, of course, inevitable that I should find out that he had not had a play produced for the last twenty years, but then the aureole of the hundred and sixty was about his poor bald head. I thought of the chances of life, he alluded to the war; and so this unpleasantness was passed over, and we entered on more genial subjects of conversation. He had written plays with everybody; his list of collaborateurs was longer than any list of lady patronesses for an English county ball; there was no literary kitchen in which he had not helped to dish up. I was at once amazed and delighted. Had M. Duval written his hundred and sixty plays in the seclusion of his own rooms, I should have been less surprised; it was the mystery of the *séances* of collaboration, the rendezvous, the discussion, the illustrious company, that overwhelmed me in a rapture of wonder and respectful admiration. Then came the anecdotes. They were of all sorts. Here are a few specimens: He, Duval, had written a one-act piece with Dumas *père*; it had been refused at the Français, and then it had been about, here, there, and everywhere; finally the *Variétés* had asked for some alterations, and *c'était une affaire entendue*. "I made the alterations one afternoon, and wrote to Dumas, and what do you think,—by return of post I had a letter from him saying he could not consent to the production of a one-act piece, signed by him, at the *Variétés,* because his son was then giving a five-act piece at the Gymnase." Then came a string of indecent witticisms by Suzanne Lagier and Dejazet. They were as old as the world, but they were new to me, and I was amused and astonished. These *bon-mots* were followed by an account of how Gautier wrote his Sunday feuilleton, and how he and Balzac had once nearly come to blows. They had agreed to collaborate. Balzac was to contribute the scenario, Gautier the dialogue. One morning Balzac came with the scenario of the first act. "Here it is, Gautier! I suppose you can let me have it back finished by tomorrow afternoon?" And the old gentleman would chirp along in this fashion till midnight. I would then accompany him to his rooms in the Quartier Montmartre—rooms high up on the fifth floor—where, between two pictures, supposed to be by Angelica Kauffmann, M. Duval had written unactable plays for the last twenty years, and where he would continue to write unactable plays until God called him to a world, perhaps, of eternal cantatas, but where, by all accounts, *l'exposition de la pièce selon la formule de M. Scribe* is still unknown.

How I used to enjoy these conversations! I remember how I used to stand on the pavement after having bid the old gentleman goodnight, regretting I had not asked for some further explanation regarding *le mouvement Romantique*, or *la façon de M. Scribe de ménager la situation*.

Why not write a comedy? So the thought came. I had never written anything save a few ill-spelt letters; but no matter. To find a plot was the first thing. Take Marshall for hero and Alice for heroine, surround them with the old gentlemen who dined at the *table d'hôte,* flavour with the Italian countess who smoked cigars when there were not too many strangers present. After three weeks of industrious stirring, the ingredients did begin to simmer into something resembling a plot. Put it upon paper. Ah! there was my difficulty. I remembered suddenly that I had read "Cain," "Manfred," "The Cenci," as poems, without ever thinking of how the dialogue looked upon paper; besides, they were in blank verse. I hadn't a notion how prose dialogue would look upon paper. Shakespeare I had never opened; no instinctive want had urged me to read him. He had remained, therefore, unread, unlooked at. Should I buy a copy? No; the name repelled me—as all popular names repelled me. In preference I went to the Gymnase, and listened attentively to a comedy by M. Dumas *fils*. But strain my imagination as I would, I could not see the spoken words in their written form. Oh, for a look at the prompter's copy, the corner of which I could see when I leaned forward! At last I discovered in Galignani's library a copy of Leigh Hunt's edition of the old dramatists, and after a month's study of Congreve, Wycherley, Vanbrugh, and Farquhar, I completed a comedy in three acts, which I entitled "Worldliness." It was, of course, very bad;

but, if my memory serves me well, I do not think it was nearly so bad as might be imagined.

No sooner was the last scene written than I started at once for London, confident I should find no difficulty in getting my play produced.

IV

I s it necessary to say that I did not find a manager to produce my play? A printer was more obtainable, and the correction of proofs amused me for a while. I wrote another play; and when the hieing after theatrical managers began to lose its attractiveness my thoughts reverted to France, which always haunted me; and which now possessed me as if with the sweet and magnetic influence of home.

How important my absence from Paris seemed to me; and how Paris rushed into my eyes!—Paris—public ball-rooms, *cafés*, the models in the studio and the young girls painting, and Marshall, Alice and Julien. Marshall!—my thoughts pointed at him through the intervening streets and the endless procession of people coming and going.

"M. Marshall, is he at home?" "M. Marshall left here some months ago." "Do you know his address?" "I'll ask my husband." "Do you know M. Marshall's address?" "Yes, he's gone to live in the Rue de Douai." "What number?" "I think it is fifty—four." "Thanks." "Coachman, wake up; drive me to the Rue de Douai."

But Marshall was not to be found at the Rue de Douai; and he had left no address. There was nothing for it but to go to the studio; I should be able to obtain news of him there—perhaps find him. But when I pulled aside the curtain, the accustomed piece of slim nakedness did not greet my eyes, only the blue apron of an old woman enveloped in a cloud of dust. "The gentlemen are not here today, the studio is closed, I am sweeping up." "Oh, and where is M. Julien?" "I cannot say, sir: perhaps at the *café*, or perhaps he is gone to the country." This was not very encouraging, and now, my enthusiasm thoroughly damped, I strolled along *le Passage*, looking at the fans, the bangles and the litter of cheap trinkets that each window was filled with. On the left at the corner of the Boulevard was our *café*. As I came forward the waiter moved one of the tin tables, and then I saw the fat Provençal. But just as if he had seen me yesterday he said, "*Tiens! c'est vous; une demi-tasse? oui. . . garçon, une demi-tasse.*" Presently the conversation turned on Marshall; they had not seen much of him lately. "*Il paraît qu'il est plus amoureux que jamais,*" Julien replied sardonically.

V

I found my friend in large furnished apartments on the ground floor in the Rue Duphot. The walls were stretched with blue silk, there were large mirrors and great gilt cornices. Passing into the bedroom I found the young god wallowing in the finest of fine linen—in a great Louis XV bed, and there were cupids above him. "Holloa! what, you back again, George Moore? we thought we weren't going to see you again."

"It's nearly one o'clock; get up. What's the news?"

"Today is the opening of the exhibition of the Impressionists. We'll have a bit of breakfast round the corner, at Durant's, and we'll go on there. I hear that Bedlam is nothing to it; there is a canvas there twenty feet square and in three tints: pale yellow for the sunlight, brown for the shadows, and all the rest is sky-blue. There is, I am told, a lady walking in the foreground with a ring-tailed monkey, and the tail is said to be three yards long."

We went to jeer a group of enthusiasts that willingly forfeit all delights of the world in the hope of realising a new æstheticism; we went insolent with patent leather shoes and bright kid gloves and armed with all the jargon of the school. "*Cette jambe ne porte pas*"; "*la nature ne se fait pas comme ça*"; "*on dessine par les masses; combien de têtes?*" "*Sept et demi.*" "*Si j'avais un morceau de craie je mettrais celle-là dans un; bocal c'est un fœtus*"; in a word, all that the journals of culture are pleased to term an artistic education. We indulged in boisterous laughter, exaggerated in the hope of giving as much pain as possible, and deep down in our souls we knew that we were lying—at least I did.

In the beginning of this century the tradition of French art—the tradition of Boucher, Fragonard, and Watteau—had been completely lost; having produced genius, their art died. Ingres is the sublime flower of the classic art which succeeded the art of the palace and the boudoir: further than Ingres it was impossible to go, and his art died. Then the Turners and Constables came to France, and they begot Troyon, and Troyon begot Millet, Courbet, Corot, and Rousseau, and these in turn begot Degas, Pissarro, Madame Morizot and Guillaumin. Degas is a pupil of Ingres, but he applies the marvellous acuteness of drawing he learned from his master to delineating the humblest aspects of modern life. Degas draws not by the masses, but by the character;—his subjects are shop-girls, ballet-girls, and washerwomen, but the qualities that endow them with immortality are precisely those which eternalise the virgins and saints of Leonardo da Vinci in the minds of men. You see the fat, vulgar woman in the long cloak trying on a hat in front of the pier-glass. So marvellously well are the lines of her face observed and rendered that you can tell exactly what her position in life is; you know what the furniture of her rooms is like; you know what she would say to you if she were to speak. She is as typical of the nineteenth century as Fragonard's ladies are of the Court of Louis XV. To the right you see a picture of two shop-girls with bonnets in their hands. So accurately are the habitual movements of the heads and the hands observed that you at once realise the years of bonnet-showing and servile words that these women have lived through. We have seen Degas do this before—it is a welcome repetition of a familiar note, but it is not until we turn to the set of nude figures that we find the great artist revealing any new phase of his talent. The first, in an attitude which suggests the kneeling Venus, washes her thighs in a tin bath. The second, a back view, full of the malformations of forty years, of children, of hard work, stands gripping her flanks with both hands. The naked woman has become impossible in modern art; it required Degas' genius to infuse new life into the worn-out theme. Cynicism was the great means of eloquence of the middle ages, and with cynicism Degas has rendered the nude again an artistic possibility. What Mr. Horsley or the British matron would say it is difficult to guess. Perhaps the hideousness depicted by M. Degas would frighten them more than the sensuality which they condemn in Sir Frederick Leighton. But, be this as it may, it is certain that the great, fat, short-legged creature, who in her humble and touching ugliness passes a chemise over her lumpy shoulders, is a triumph of art. Ugliness is trivial, the monstrous is terrible; Velasquez knew this when he painted his dwarfs.

Pissarro exhibited a group of girls gathering apples in a garden—sad greys and violets beautifully harmonised. The figures seem to move as in a dream: we are on the thither side of life, in a world of quiet colour and happy aspiration. Those apples will never fall from the branches, those baskets that the stooping girls are filling will never be filled: that garden is the garden of the peace that life has not for giving, but which the painter has set in an eternal dream of violet and grey.

Madame Morizot exhibited a series of delicate fancies. Here are two young girls, the sweet atmosphere folds them as with a veil, they are all summer, their dreams are limitless, their days are fading, and their ideas follow the flight of the white butterflies through the standard roses. Take note, too, of the stand of fans; what delicious fancies are there—willows, balconies, gardens, and terraces.

Then, contrasting with these distant tendernesses, there was the vigorous painting of Guillaumin. There life is rendered in violent and colourful brutality. The ladies fishing in the park, with the violet of the skies and the green of the trees descending upon them, is a *chef d'œuvre.* Nature seems to be closing about them like a tomb; and that hillside,—sunset flooding the skies with yellow and the earth with blue shadow,—is another piece of painting that will one day find a place in one of the public galleries; and the same can be said of the portrait of the woman on a background of chintz flowers.

We could but utter coarse gibes and exclaim, "What could have induced him to paint such things? surely he must have seen that it was absurd. I wonder if the Impressionists are in earnest or if it is only *une blague qu'on nous fait?*" Then we stood and screamed at Monet, that most exquisite painter of blonde light. We stood before the "Turkeys," and seriously we wondered if "it was serious work,"—that *chef d'œuvre!* the high grass that the turkeys are gobbling is flooded with sunlight so swift and intense that for a moment the illusion is complete. "Just look at the house! why, the turkeys couldn't walk in at the door. The perspective is all wrong." Then followed other remarks of an educational kind; and when we came to those piercingly personal visions of railway stations by the same painter,—those rapid sensations of steel and vapour,—our laughter knew no bounds. "I say, Marshall, just look at this wheel; he dipped his brush into cadmium yellow and whisked it round, that's all." Nor had we anymore understanding for Renoir's rich sensualities of tone; nor did the mastery with which he achieves an absence of shadow appeal to us. You see colour and light in his pictures as you do in nature, and the child's criticism of a portrait—"Why is one side of the face black?" is answered. There was a half-length nude figure of a girl. How the round fresh breasts palpitate in the light! such a glorious glow of whiteness was attained never before. But we saw nothing except that the eyes were out of drawing.

For art was not for us then as it is now,—a mere emotion, right or wrong only in proportion to its intensity; we believed then in the grammar of art, perspective, anatomy, and *la jambe qui porte*; and we found all this in Julien's studio.

A year passed; a year of art and dissipation—one part art, two parts dissipation. We mounted and descended at pleasure the rounds of society's ladder. One evening we would spend at Constant's, Rue de la Gaieté, in the company of thieves and housebreakers; on the following evening we were dining with a duchess or a princess in the Champs Elysées. And we prided ourselves vastly on our versatility in using with equal facility the language of the "fence's" parlour, and that of the literary *salon*; on being able to appear as much at home in one as in the other. Delighted at our prowess, we often whispered, "The princess, I swear, would not believe her eyes if she saw us now"; and then in terrible slang we shouted a benediction on some "crib" that was going to be broken into that evening. And we thought there was something very thrilling in leaving the Rue de la Gaieté, returning home to dress, and presenting our spotless selves to the *élite*. And we succeeded very well, as indeed all young men do who waltz perfectly and avoid making love to the wrong woman.

But the excitement of climbing up and down the social ladder did not stave off our craving for art; and about this time there came a very decisive event in our lives. Marshall's last and really *grande passion* had come to a violent termination, and monetary difficulties forced him to turn his thoughts to painting on china as a means of livelihood. And as this young man always sought extremes he went to Belleville, donned a blouse, ate garlic with his food, and settled down to live there as a workman. I had been to see him, and had found him building a wall. And with sorrow I related his state that evening to Julien in the Café Veron. He said, after a pause:—

"Since you profess so much friendship for him, why do you not do him a service that cannot be forgotten since the result will always continue? why don't you save him from the life you describe? If you are not actually rich you are at least in easy circumstances, and can afford to give him a *pension* of three hundred francs a month. I will give him the use of my studio, which means, as you know, models and teaching; Marshall has plenty of talent, all he wants is a year's education: in a year or a year-and-a-half, certainly at the end of two years, he will begin to make money."

It is rather a shock to one who is at all concerned with his own genius to be asked to act as foster-mother to another's. Then three hundred francs meant a great deal, plainly it meant deprivation of those superfluities which are so intensely necessary to the delicate and refined. Julien watched me. This large crafty Southerner knew what was passing in me; he knew I was realising all the manifold inconveniences—the duty of looking after Marshall's wants for two years, and to make the pill easier he said:—

"If three hundred francs a month are too heavy for your purse, you might take an apartment and ask Marshall to come and live with you. You told me the other day you were tired of hotel life. It would be an advantage to you to live with him. You want to do something yourself; and the fact of his being obliged to attend the studio (for I should advise you to have a strict agreement with him regarding the work he is to do) would be an extra inducement to you to work hard."

I always decide at once, reflection does not help me, and a moment after I said, "Very well, Julien, I will."

And next day I went with the news to Belleville. Marshall protested he had no real talent. I protested he had. The agreement was drawn up and signed. He was to work in the studio eight hours a day; he was to draw until such time as M. Lefebvre set him to paint; and in proof of his industry he was to bring me at the end of each week a study from life and a composition, the subject of which the master gave at the beginning of each week, and in return I was to take an apartment near the studio, give him an abode, food, *blanchissage*, etc. Once the matter was decided, Marshall manifested prodigious energy, and three days after he told me he had found an apartment in Le Passage des Panoramas which would suit us perfectly. The plunge had to be taken. I paid my hotel bill, and sent my taciturn valet to beef, beer and a wife.

It was unpleasant to have a window opening not to the sky, but to an unclean prospect of glass roofing; nor was it agreeable to get up at seven in the morning; and ten hours of work daily are trying to the resolution even of the best intentioned. But we had sworn to forego all pleasures for the sake of art—*table d'hôtes* in the Rue Maubeuge, French and foreign duchesses in the Champs Elysées, thieves in the Rue de la Gaieté.

I was entering therefore on a duel with Marshall for supremacy in an art for which, as has already been said, I possessed no qualifications. It will readily be understood how a mind like mine, so intensely alive to all impulses, and so unsupported by any moral convictions, would suffer in so keen a contest waged under such unequal and cruel conditions. It was in truth a year of great passion and great despair. Defeat is bitter when it comes swiftly and conclusively, but when defeat falls by inches like the pendulum in the pit, the agony is a little beyond verbal expression. I remember the first day of my martyrdom. The clocks were striking eight; we chose our places, got into position. After the first hour, I compared my drawing with Marshall's. He had, it is true, caught the movement of the figure better than I, but the character and the quality of his work was miserable. That of mine was not. I have said I possessed no artistic facility, but I did not say faculty; my drawing was never common; it was individual in feeling, it was refined. I possessed all the rarer qualities, but not that primary power without which all is valueless;—I mean the talent of the boy who can knock off a clever caricature of his school-master or make a *lifelike* sketch of his favourite horse on the barn door with a piece of chalk.

The following week Marshall made a great deal of progress; I thought the model did not suit me, and hoped for better luck next time. That time never came, and at the end of the first month I was left toiling hopelessly in the distance. Marshall's mind, though shallow, was bright, and he understood with strange ease all that was told him, and was able to put into immediate practice the methods of work inculcated by the professors. In fact, he showed himself singularly capable of education; little could be drawn out, but a great deal could be put in (using the word in its modern, not in its original sense). He showed himself intensely anxious to learn and to accept all that was said: the ideas and feelings of others ran into him like water into a bottle whose neck is suddenly stooped below the surface of the stream. He was an ideal pupil. It was Marshall here, it was Marshall there, and soon the studio was little but an agitation in praise of him, and his work, and anxious speculation arose as to the medals he would obtain. I continued the struggle for nine months. I was in the studio at eight in the morning, I measured my drawing, I plumbed it throughout, I sketched in, having regard to *la jambe qui porte*, I modelled *par les masses*. During breakfast I considered how I should work during the afternoon, at night I lay awake thinking of what I might do to obtain a better result. But my efforts availed me nothing, it was like one who, falling, stretches his arms for help and grasps the yielding air. How terrible are the languors and yearnings of impotence! how wearing! what an aching void they leave in the heart! And all this I suffered until the burden of unachieved desire grew intolerable.

I laid down my charcoal and said, "I will never draw or paint again." That vow I have kept.

Surrender brought relief, but my life seemed at an end. I looked upon a blank space of years desolate as a grey and sailless sea. "What shall I do?" I asked myself, and my heart was weary and hopeless. Literature? my heart did not answer the question at once. I was too broken and overcome by the shock of failure; failure precise and stern, admitting of no equivocation. I strove to read: but it was impossible to sit at home almost within earshot of the studio, and with all the memories of defeat still ringing their knells in my heart. Marshall's success clamoured loudly from without; everyday, almost every hour of the day, I heard of the medals which he would carry off, of what Lefebvre thought of his drawing this week, of Boulanger's opinion of his talent. I do not wish to excuse my conduct, but I cannot help saying that Marshall showed me neither consideration nor pity, he did not even seem to understand that I was suffering, that my nerves had been terribly shaken, and he flaunted his superiority relentlessly in my face— his good looks, his talents, his popularity. I did not know then how little these studio successes really meant.

Vanity? no, it was not his vanity that maddened me; to me vanity is rarely displeasing, sometimes it is singularly attractive; but by a certain insistence and aggressiveness in the details of life he allowed me to feel that I was only a means for the moment, a serviceable thing enough, but one that would be very soon discarded and passed over. This was intolerable. I packed up my portmanteau and left, after having kept my promise for only ten months. By so doing I involved my friend in grave and cruel difficulties; by this action I imperilled his future prospects. It was a dastardly action, but his presence had grown unbearable; yes, unbearable in the fullest acceptation of the word, and in ridding myself of him I felt as if a world of misery were being lifted from me.

VI

After three months spent in a sweet seaside resort, where unoccupied men and ladies whose husbands are abroad happily congregate, I returned to Paris refreshed.

Marshall and I were no longer on speaking terms, but I saw him daily, in a new overcoat, of a cut admirably adapted to his figure, sweeping past the fans and the jet ornaments of the Passage des Panoramas. The coat interested me, and I remembered that if I had not broken with him I should have been able to ask him some essential questions concerning it. Of such trifles as this the sincerest friendships are made; he was as necessary to me as I to him, and after some demur on his part a reconciliation was effected.

Then I took an *appartement* in one of the old houses in Rue de la Tour des Dames, for windows there overlooked a bit of tangled garden with a dilapidated statue. It was Marshall of course who undertook the task of furnishing, and he lavished on the rooms the fancies of an imagination that suggested the collaboration of a courtesan of high degree and a fifth-rate artist. Nevertheless, our *salon* was a pretty resort—English cretonne of a very happy design—vine leaves, dark green and golden, broken up by many fluttering jays. The walls were stretched with this colourful cloth, and the arm-chairs and the couches were to match. The drawing-room was in cardinal red, hung from the middle of the ceiling and looped up to give the appearance of a tent; a faun, in terra-cotta, laughed in the red gloom, and there were Turkish couches and lamps. In another room you faced an altar, a Buddhist temple, a statue of the Apollo, and a bust of Shelley. The bedrooms were made unconventual with cushioned seats and rich canopies; and in picturesque corners there were censers, great church candlesticks, and palms; then think of the smell of burning incense and wax and you will have imagined the sentiment of our apartment in Rue de la Tour des Dames. I bought a Persian cat, and a python that made a monthly meal off guinea pigs; Marshall, who did not care for pets, filled his rooms with flowers—he used to sleep beneath a tree of gardenias in full bloom. We were so, Henry Marshall and George Moore, when we went to live in 76 Rue de la Tour des Dames, we hoped for the rest of our lives. He was to paint, I was to write.

Before leaving for the seaside I had bought some volumes of Hugo and De Musset; but in pleasant, sunny Boulogne poetry went flat, and it was not until I got into my new rooms that I began to read seriously. Books are like individuals; you know at once if they are going to create a sense within the sense, to fever, to madden you in blood and brain, or if they will merely leave you indifferent, or irritable, having unpleasantly disturbed sweet intimate musings as might a draught from an open window. Many are the reasons for love, but I confess I only love woman or book, when it is as a voice of conscience, never heard before, heard suddenly, a voice I am at once endearingly intimate with. This announces feminine depravities in my affections. I am feminine, morbid, perverse. But above all perverse, almost everything perverse interests, fascinates me. Wordsworth is the only simple-minded man I ever loved, if that great austere mind, chill even as the Cumberland year, can be called simple. But Hugo is not perverse, nor even personal. Reading him was like being in church with a strident-voiced preacher shouting from out of a terribly sonorous pulpit. "Les Orientales. . ." An East of painted cardboard, tin daggers, and a military band playing the Turkish patrol in the Palais Royal. . . The verse is grand, noble, tremendous; I liked it, I admired it, but it did not—I repeat the phrase—awake a voice of conscience within me; and even the structure of the verse was too much in the style of public buildings to please me. Of "Les Feuilles d'Automne" and "Les Chants du Crépuscule" I remember nothing. Ten lines, fifty lines of "Les Légendes des Siècles," and I always think that it is the greatest poetry I have ever read, but after a few pages the book is laid down and forgotten. Having composed more verses than any man that ever lived, Hugo can only be taken in the smallest doses; if you repeat any passage to a friend across a *café* table, you are both appalled by the splendour of the imagery, by the thunder of the syllables.

> *"Quel dieu, quel moissonneur de l'éternel été*
> *Avait en s'en allant négligemment jeté*
> *Cette faucille d'or dans les champs des étoiles."*

But if I read an entire poem I never escape that sensation of the *ennui* which is inherent in the gaud and the glitter of the Italian or Spanish improvisatore. There never was anything French about Hugo's genius. Hugo was a cross between an Italian improvisatore and a metaphysical German student. Take another verse—

"Le clair de lune bleu qui baigne l'horizon."

Without a "like" or an "as," by a mere statement of fact, the picture, nay more, the impression, is produced. I confess I have a weakness for the poem which this line concludes—"La fête chez Thérèse"; but admirable as it is with its picture of mediæval life, there is in it, as in all Hugo's work, a sense of fabrication that dries up emotion in my heart. He shouts and raves over poor humanity, while he is gathering coppers for himself; he goes in for an all-round patronage of the Almighty in a last stanza; but of the two immortalities he evidently considers his own the most durable; he does not, however, become really intolerable until he gets on the subject of little children, he sings their innocence in great bombast, but he is watching them; the poetry over, the crowd dispersed, he will entice one of them down a byway.

The first time I read of *une bouche d'ombre* I was astonished, nor did the second or third repetition produce a change in my mood of mind; but sooner or later it was impossible to avoid conviction, that of the two "the rosy fingers of the dawn," although some three thousand years older is younger, truer, and more beautiful. Homer's similes can never grow old; *une bouche d'ombre* was old the first time it was said. It is the birthplace and the grave of Hugo's genius.

Of Alfred de Musset I had heard a great deal. Marshall and the Marquise were in the habit of reading him in moments of relaxation, they had marked their favourite passages, so he came to me highly recommended. Nevertheless, I made but little progress in his poetry. His modernisms were out of tune with the strain of my aspirations at that moment, and I did not find the unexpected word and the eccentricities of expression which were, and are still, so dear to me. I am not a purist; an error of diction is very pardonable if it does not err on the side of the commonplace; the commonplace, the natural, is constitutionally abhorrent to me; and I have never been able to read with any very thorough sense of pleasure even the opening lines of "Rolla," that splendid lyrical outburst. What I remember of it now are those two odious *chevilles—marchait et respirait*, and *Astarté fille de l'onde amère*; nor does the fact that *amère* rhymes with *mère* condone the offence, although it proves that even Musset felt that perhaps the richness of the rhyme might render tolerable the intolerable. And it is to my credit that the Spanish love songs moved me not at all; and it was not until I read that magnificently grotesque poem "La Ballade à la Lune," that I could be induced to bend the knee and acknowledge Musset a poet.

I still read and spoke of Shelley with a rapture of joy,—he was still my soul. But this craft, fashioned of mother-o'-pearl, with starlight at the helm and moonbeams for sails, suddenly ran on a reef and went down, not out of sight, but out of the agitation of actual life. The reef was Gautier; I read "Mdlle. de Maupin." The reaction was as violent as it was sudden. I was weary of spiritual passion, and this great exaltation of the body above the soul at once conquered and led me captive; this plain scorn of a world as exemplified in lacerated saints and a crucified Redeemer opened up to me illimitable prospects of fresh beliefs, and therefore new joys in things and new revolts against all that had come to form part and parcel of the commonalty of mankind. Till now I had not even remotely suspected that a deification of flesh and fleshly desire was possible, Shelley's teaching had been, while accepting the body, to dream of the soul as a star, and so preserve our ideal; but now suddenly I saw, with delightful clearness and with intoxicating conviction, that by looking without shame and accepting with love the flesh, I might raise it to as high a place within as divine a light as even the soul had been set in. The ages were as an aureole, and I stood as if enchanted before the noble nakedness of the elder gods: not the infamous nudity that sex has preserved in this modern world, but the clean pagan nude,—a love of life and beauty, the broad fair breast of a boy, the long flanks, the head thrown back; the bold fearless gaze of Venus is lovelier than the lowered glance of the Virgin, and I cried with my master that the blood that flowed upon Mount Calvary "*ne m'a jamais baigné dans ses flots.*"

I will not turn to the book to find the exact words of this sublime vindication, for ten years I have not read the Word that has become so inexpressibly a part of me; and shall I not refrain as Mdlle. de Maupin refrained, knowing well that the face of love may not be twice seen? Great was my conversion. None more than I had cherished mystery and dream: my life until now had been but a mist which revealed as each cloud wreathed and went out, the red of some strange flower or some tall peak, blue and snowy and fairylike in lonely moonlight; and now so great was my conversion that the more brutal the outrage offered to my ancient ideal, the rarer and keener was my delight. I read almost without fear: "My dreams were of naked youths riding white horses through mountain passes, there were no clouds in my dreams, or if there were any, they were clouds that had been cut out as if in cardboard with scissors."

I had shaken off all belief in Christianity early in life and had suffered much. Shelley had replaced faith by reason, but I still suffered: but here was a new creed which proclaimed the divinity of the body, and for a long time the reconstruction of all my theories of life on a purely pagan basis occupied my whole attention. The exquisite outlines of the marvellous castle, the romantic woods, the horses moving, the lovers leaning to each other's faces enchanted me; and then the indescribably beautiful description of the performance of *As You Like It*, and the supreme relief and perfect assuagement it brings to Rodolph, who then sees Mdlle. de Maupin for the first time in woman's attire. If she were dangerously beautiful as a man, that beauty is forgotten in the rapture and praise of her unmatchable woman's loveliness.

But if "Mdlle. de Maupin" was the highest peak, it was not the entire mountain. The range was long, and each summit offered to the eye a new and delightful prospect. There were the numerous tales,—tales as perfect as the world has ever seen; "La Morte Amoureuse," "Jettatura," "Une Nuit de Cléopâtre," etc., and then the very diamonds of the crown, "Les Emaux et Camées," "La Symphonie en Blanc Majeure," in which the adjective *blanc* and *blanche* is repeated with miraculous felicity in each stanza. And then Contralto,—

> *"Mais seulement il se transpose*
> *Et passant de la forme au son,*
> *Trouve dans la métamorphose*
> *La jeune fille et le garçon."*

Transpose,—a word never before used except in musical application, and now for the first time applied to material form, and with a beauty-giving touch that Phidias might be proud of. I know not how I quote; such is my best memory of the stanza, and here, that is more important than the stanza itself. And that other stanza, "The Châtelaine and the Page"; and that other, "The Doves"; and that other, "Romeo and Juliet," and the exquisite cadence of the line ending "*balcon*." Novelists have often shown how a love passion brings misery, despair, death and ruin upon a life, but I know of no story of the good or evil influence awakened by the chance reading of a book, the chain of consequences so far-reaching, so intensely dramatic. Never shall I open these books again, but were

I to live for a thousand years, their power in my soul would remain unshaken. I am what they made me. Belief in humanity, pity for the poor, hatred of injustice, all that Shelley gave may never have been very deep or earnest; but I did love, I did believe. Gautier destroyed these illusions. He taught me that our boasted progress is but a pitfall into which the race is falling, and I learned that the correction of form is the highest ideal, and I accepted the plain, simple conscience of the pagan world as the perfect solution of the problem that had vexed me so long; I cried, "ave" to it all: lust, cruelty, slavery, and I would have held down my thumbs in the Colosseum that a hundred gladiators might die and wash me free of my Christian soul with their blood.

The study of Baudelaire hurried the course of the disease. [1] No longer is it the grand barbaric face of Gautier; now it is the clean shaven face of the mock priest, the slow, cold eyes and the sharp, cunning sneer of the cynical libertine who will be tempted that he may better know the worthlessness of temptation. "Les Fleurs du Mal!" beautiful flowers, beautiful in sublime decay. What a great record is yours, and were Hell a reality how many souls would we find wreathed with your poisonous blossoms. The village maiden goes to her Faust; the children of the nineteenth century go to you, O Baudelaire, and having tasted of your deadly delight all hope of repentance is vain. Flowers, beautiful in your sublime decay, I press you to my lips; these northern solitudes, far from the rank Parisian garden where I gathered you, are full of you, even as the sea-shell of the sea, and the sun that sets on this wild moorland evokes the magical verse:—

"Un soir fait de rose et de bleu mystique
Nous échangerons un éclair unique
Comme un long sanglot tout chargé d'adieux."

For months I fed on the mad and morbid literature that the enthusiasm of 1830 called into existence. The gloomy and sterile little pictures of "Gaspard de la Nuit," or the elaborate criminality, "Les Contes Immoraux," laboriously invented lifeless things with creaky joints, pitiful lay figures that fall to dust as soon as the book is closed, and in the dust only the figures of the terrible ferryman and the unfortunate

---

1. Surely the phrase is ill considered, hurried "my convalescence" would express the author's meaning better.

Dora remain. "Madame Potiphar" cost me forty francs, and I never read more than a few pages.

Like a pike after minnows I pursued the works of Les Jeune France along the quays and through every *passage* in Paris. The money spent was considerable, the waste of time vexatious. One man's solitary work (he died very young, but he is known to have excelled all in length of his hair and the redness of his waistcoats) resisted my efforts to capture it. At last I caught sight of the precious volume in a shop on the Quai Voltaire. Trembling I asked the price. The man looked at me earnestly and answered, "A hundred and fifty francs." No doubt it was a great deal of money, but I paid it and rushed home to read. Many that had gone before had proved disappointing, and I was obliged to admit had contributed little towards my intellectual advancement; but this—this that I had heard about so long—not a queer phrase, not an outrage of any sort of kind, not even a new blasphemy, it meant nothing to me, that is to say, nothing but a hundred and fifty francs. Having thus rudely, and very pikelike, knocked my nose against the bottom—this book was, most certainly, the bottom of the literature of 1830—I came up to the surface and began to look around my contemporaries for something to read.

I have remarked before on the instinctiveness of my likes and dislikes, on my susceptibility to the sound of and even to the appearance of a name upon paper. I was repelled by Leconte de Lisle from the first, and it was only by a very deliberate outrage to my feelings that I bought and read "Les Poèmes Antiques," and "Les Poèmes Barbares"; I was deceived in nothing, all I had anticipated I found—long, desolate boredom. Leconte de Lisle produces on me the effect of a walk through the new Law Courts, with a steady but not violent draught sweeping from end to end. Oh, the vile old professor of rhetoric! and when I saw him the last time I was in Paris, his head—a declaration of righteousness, a cross between a Cæsar by Gerome, and an archbishop of a provincial town, set all my natural antipathy instantly on edge. Hugo is often pompous, shallow, empty, unreal, but he is at least an artist, and when he thinks of the artist and forgets the prophet, as in "Les Chansons des Rues et des Bois," his juggling with the verse is magnificent, superb.

"Comme un geai sur l'arbre
Le roi se tient fier;
Son cœur est de marbre,
Son ventre est de chair.

"On a pour sa nuque
Et son front vermeil
Fait une perruque
Avec le soleil.

"Il règne, il végète
Effroyant zéro;
Sur lui se projette
L'ombre du bourreau.

"Son trône est une tombe,
Et sur le pavé
Quelque chose en tombe
Qu'on n'a point lavé."

But how to get the first line of the last stanza into five syllables I cannot think. If ever I meet with the volume again I will look it out and see how that *rude dompteur de syllables* managed it. But stay, *son trône est la tombe*; that makes the verse, and the generalisation would be in the "line" of Hugo. Hugo—how impossible it is to speak of French literature without referring to him. Let these, however, be concluding words that he thought he could by saying everything, and, saying everything twenty times over, forever render impossible the rehearsal of another great poet. But a work of art is valuable, and pleasurable in proportion to its rarity; one beautiful book of verses is better than twenty books of beautiful verses. This is an absolute and incontestable truth; a child can burlesque this truth—one verse is better than the whole poem, a word is better than the line, a letter is better than the word, but the truth is not thereby affected. Hugo never had the good fortune to write a bad book, nor even a single bad line, so not having time to read all, the future will read none. What immortality would be gained by the destruction of one half of his magnificent works, what oblivion is secured by the publication of these posthumous volumes.

To return to the Leconte de Lisle. See his "Discours de Réception." Is it possible to imagine anything more absurdly arid? Rhetoric of this sort, "*des vers d'or sur une éclume d'airain*" and such sententious platitudes as this (speaking of the realists), "*Les épidémies de cette nature passent, et le génie demeure.*"

Theodore de Banville. At first I thought him cold, infected with the rhetorical ice of the Leconte de Lisle. He had no new creed to proclaim nor old creed to denounce, the inherent miseries of human life did not seem to touch him, nor did he sing the languors and ardours of animal or spiritual passion. But there is this: a pure, clear song, an instinctive, incurable and lark-like love of the song. He sings of the white lily and the red rose, such knowledge of, such observation of nature is enough for the poet, and he sings and he trills, there is trilling magic in every song, and the song as it ascends rings, and all the air quivers with the ever-widening circle of the echoes, sighing and dying out of the ear until the last faintness is reached, and the glad rhymes clash and dash forth again on their aerial way. Banville is not the poet, he is the bard. The great questions that agitate the mind of man have not troubled him, life, death, and love he perceives only as stalks whereon he may weave his glittering web of living words. Whatever his moods may be, he is lyrical. His wit flies out on clear-cut, swallow-like wings; in speaking of Paul Alexis' book "Le Besoin d'aimer," he said: *"Vous avez trouvé un titre assez laid pour faire reculer les divines étoiles."* I know not what instrument to compare with his verse. I suppose I should say a flute; but it seems to me more like a marvellously toned piano. His hands pass over the keys and he produces Chopin-like fluidities.

It is now well known that French verse is not seventy years old. If it was Hugo who invented French rhyme it was Banville who broke up the couplet. Hugo had perhaps ventured to place the pause between the adjective and its noun, but it was not until Banville wrote the line, *"Elle filait pensivement la blanche laine"* that the cæsura received its final *coup de grâce*. This verse has been probably more imitated than any other verse in the French language. *Pensivement* was replaced by some similar four-syllable adverb, *Elle tirait nonchalamment les bas de soie, etc*. It was the beginning of the end.

I read the French poets of the modern school—Coppée, Mendés, Léon Diex, Verlaine, José Maria Hêrédia, Mallarmé, Richepin, Villiers de l'Isle Adam. Coppée, as may be imagined, I only was capable of appreciating in his first manner, when he wrote those exquisite but purely artistic sonnets "La Tulipe," and "Le Lys." In the latter a room decorated with daggers, armour, jewellery and china is beautifully described, and it is only in the last line that the lily, which animates and gives life to the whole, is introduced. But the exquisite poetic perceptivity Coppée showed in his modern poems, the certainty with which he raised the commonest subject, investing it with sufficient dignity for his purpose, escaped me wholly, and I could not but turn with horror from such poems as "La Nourrice" and "Le Petit Epicier." How anyone could bring himself to acknowledge the vulgar details of our vulgar age I could not understand. The fiery glory of José Maria de Hérédia, on the contrary, filled me with enthusiasm—ruins and sand, shadow and silhouette of palms and pillars, negroes, crimson, swords, silence, and arabesques. Like great copper pans go the clangour of the rhymes.

> *"Entre le ciel qui brûle et la mer qui moutonne,*
> *Au somnolent soleil d'un midi monotone,*
> *Tu songes, O guerrière, aux vieux conquistadors;*
> *Et dans l'énervement des nuits chaudes et calmes,*
> *Berçant ta gloire éteinte, O cité, tu t'endors*
> *Sous les palmiers, au long frémissement des palmes."*

Catulle Mendès, a perfect realisation of his name, with his pale hair, and his fragile face illuminated with the idealism of a depraved woman. He takes you by the arm, by the hand, he leans towards you, his words are caresses, his fervour is delightful, and to hear him is as sweet as drinking a smooth perfumed yellow wine. All he says is false—the book he has just read, the play he is writing, the woman who loves him, . . . he buys a packet of bonbons in the streets and eats them, and it is false. An exquisite artist; physically and spiritually he is art; he is the muse herself, or rather, he is one of the minions of the muse. Passing from flower to flower he goes, his whole nature pulsing with butterfly voluptuousness. He has written poems as good as Hugo, as good as Leconte de Lisle, as good as Banville, as good as Baudelaire, as good as Gautier, as good as Coppée; he never wrote an ugly line in his life, but he never wrote a line that someone of his brilliant contemporaries might not have written. He has produced good work of all kinds "et voilà tout." Every generation, every country, has its Catulle Mendès. Robert Buchanan is ours, only in the adaptation Scotch gruel has been substituted for perfumed yellow wine. No more delightful talker than Mendès, no more accomplished *littérateur*, no more fluent and translucid critic. I remember the great moonlights of the *Place Pigale*, when, on leaving the *café*, he would take me by the arm, and expound Hugo's or Zola's last book, thinking as he spoke of the Greek sophists. There were for contrast Mallarmé's

Tuesday evenings, a few friends sitting round the hearth, the lamp on the table. I have met none whose conversation was more fruitful, but with the exception of his early verses I cannot say I ever enjoyed his poetry frankly. When I knew him he had published the celebrated "L'Après Midi d'un Faun": the first poem written in accordance with the theory of symbolism. But when it was given to me (this marvellous brochure furnished with strange illustrations and wonderful tassels), I thought it absurdly obscure. Since then, however, it has been rendered by force of contrast with the enigmas the author has since published a marvel of lucidity; I am sure if I were to read it now I should appreciate its many beauties. It bears the same relation to the author's later work as *Rienzi* to *The Walkyrie*. But what is symbolism? Vulgarly speaking, saying the opposite to what you mean. For example, you want to say that music which is the new art, is replacing the old art, which is poetry. First symbol: a house in which there is a funeral, the pall extends over the furniture. The house is poetry, poetry is dead. Second symbol: "*notre vieux grimoire*," *grimoire* is the parchment, parchment is used for writing, therefore, *grimoire* is the symbol for literature, "*d'où s'exaltent les milliers*," thousands of what? of letters of course. We have heard a great deal in England of Browning obscurity. The "Red Cotton Nightcap Country" is a child at play compared to a sonnet by such a determined symbolist as Mallarmé, or better still his disciple Ghil who has added to the infirmities of symbolism those of poetic instrumentation. For according to M. Ghil and his organ *Les Ecrits pour l'Art*, it would appear that the syllables of the French language evoke in us the sensations of different colours; consequently the timbre of the different instruments. The vowel *u* corresponds to the colour yellow, and therefore to the sound of flutes. Arthur Rimbaud was, it is true, first in the field with these pleasant and genial theories; but M. Ghil informs us that Rimbaud was mistaken in many things, particularly in coupling the sound of the vowel *u* with the colour green instead of with the colour yellow. M. Ghil has corrected this very stupid blunder and many others; and his instrumentation in his last volume, "Le Geste Ingénu," may be considered as complete and definitive. The work is dedicated to Mallarmé, "Père et seigneur des ors, des pierreries, et des poisons," and other works are to follow:—the six tomes of "Légendes de Rêves et de Sang," the innumerable tomes of "La Glose," and the single tome of "La Loi."

And that man Gustave Kahn, who takes the French language

as a violin, and lets the bow of his emotion run at wild will upon it, producing strange acute strains, unpremeditated harmonies comparable to nothing that I know of but some Hungarian rhapsody; verses of seventeen syllables interwoven with verses of eight, and even nine, masculine rhymes, seeking strange union with feminine rhymes in the middle of the line—a music sweet, subtil, and epicene; the half-note, the inflexion, but not the full tone—as "*se fondre, o souvenir, des lys âcres délices.*"

Se penchant vers les dahlias,
Des paons cabrent des rosaces lunaires
L'assou pissement des branches vénère
Son pâle visage aux mourants dahlias.

Elle écoute au loin les brèves musiques
Nuit claire aux ramures d'accords,
Et la lassitude a bercé son corps
Au rhythme odorant des pures musiques.

Les paons ont dressé la rampe occellée
Pour la descente de ses yeux vers le tapis
De choses et de sens
Qui va vers l'horizon, parure vermiculée
De son corps alangui
En l'âme se tapit
Le flou désir molli de récits et d'encens.

I laughed at these verbal eccentricities, but they were not without their effect, and that a demoralising one; for in me they aggravated the fever of the unknown, and whetted my appetite for the strange, abnormal and unhealthy in art. Hence all pallidities of thought and desire were eagerly welcomed, and Verlaine became my poet. Never shall I forget the first enchantment of "Les Fétes Galantes." Here all is twilight.

The royal magnificences of the sunset have passed, the solemn beatitude of the night is at hand but not yet here; the ways are veiled with shadow, and lit with dresses, white, that the hour has touched with blue, yellow, green, mauve, and undecided purple; the voices? strange contraltos; the forms? not those of men or women, but mystic, hybrid creatures, with hands nervous and pale, and eyes charged with eager and fitful light. . . "*un soir équivoque d'automne*" . . . "*les belles pendent rêveuses à nos bras*" . . . and they whisper "*les mots spéciaux et tout bas.*"

Gautier sang to his antique lyre praise of the flesh and contempt of the soul; Baudelaire on a mediæval organ chaunted his unbelief in goodness and truth and his hatred of life. But Verlaine advances one step further: hate is to him as commonplace as love, unfaith as vulgar as faith. The world is merely a doll to be attired today in a modern ball dress, tomorrow in aureoles and stars. The Virgin is a pretty thing, worth a poem, but it would be quite too silly to talk about belief or unbelief; Christ in wood or plaster we have heard too much of, but Christ in painted glass amid crosiers and Latin terminations, is an amusing subject for poetry. And strangely enough, a withdrawing from all commerce with virtue and vice is, it would seem, a licentiousness more curiously subtle and penetrating than any other; and the licentiousness of the verse is equal to that of the emotion; every natural instinct of the language is violated, and the simple music native in French metre is replaced by falsetto notes sharp and intense. The charm is that of an odour of iris exhaled by some ideal tissues, or of a missal in a gold case, a precious relic of the pomp and ritual of an archbishop of Persepolis.

Parsifal a vaincu les filles, leur gentil
Babil et la luxure amusante et sa pente
Vers la chair de garçon vierge que cela tente
D'aimer des seins légers et ce gentil babil.

Il a vaincu la femme belle aucœur subtil
Etalant ces bras frais et sa gorge excitante;
Il a vaincu l'enfer, il rentre dans sa tente
Avec un lourd trophée à son bras puéril.

Avec la lance qui perça le flanc suprême
Il a guéri le roi, le voici roi lui-même.
Et prêtre du très-saint trésor essentiel;

En robe d'or il adore, gloire et symbole,
Le vase pur où resplendit le sang réel,
Et, o ces voix d'enfants chantant dans la coupole.

In English there is no sonnet so beautiful, its beauty cannot be worn away, it is as inexhaustible as a Greek marble. The hiatus in the last line was at first a little trying, but I have learned to love it. Not in Baudelaire nor even in Poe is there more beautiful poetry to be found. Poe, unread and ill-understood in America and England, here, thou art an integral part of our artistic life.

The Island o' Fay, Silence, Eleonore, were the familiar spirits of an apartment beautiful with Manets and tapestry; Swinburne and Rossetti were the English poets I read there; and in a golden bondage, I, a unit in the generation they have enslaved, clanked my fetters and trailed my golden chain, a set of stories in many various metres, to be called "Roses of Midnight." One of the characteristics of the volume was that daylight was banished from its pages. In the sensual lamplight of yellow boudoirs, or the wild moonlight of centenarian forests, my fantastic loves lived out their lives, died with the dawn which was supposed to be an awakening to consciousness of reality.

VII

A last hour of vivid blue and gold glare; but now the twilight sheds softly upon the darting jays, and only the little oval frames catch the fleeting beams. I go to the miniatures. Amid the parliamentary faces, all strictly garrotted with many-folded handkerchiefs, there is a metal frame enchased with rubies and a few emeralds. And this *chef d'œuvre* of antique workmanship surrounds a sharp, shrewdish, modern face, withal pretty. Fair she is and thin.

She is a woman of thirty—no,—she is the woman of thirty. Balzac has written some admirable pages on this subject; my memory of them is vague and uncertain, although durable, as all memories of him must be. But that marvellous story, or rather study, has been blunted in my knowledge of this tiny face with the fine masses of hair drawn up from the neck and arranged elaborately on the crown. There is no fear of plagiary; he cannot have said all; he cannot have said what I want to say.

Looking at this face so mundane, so intellectually mundane, I see why a young man of refined mind—a bachelor who spends at least a pound a day on his pleasures, and in whose library are found some few volumes of modern poetry—seeks his ideal in a woman of thirty.

It is clear that, by the very essence of her being, the young girl may evoke no ideal but that of home; and home is in his eyes the antithesis of freedom, desire, aspiration. He longs for mystery, deep and endless, and he is tempted with a foolish little illusion—white dresses, water-colour drawings and popular music. He dreams of Pleasure, and he is offered Duty; for do not think that that sylph-like waist does not suggest to him a yard of apron string, cries of children, and that most odious word, "Papa." A young man of refined mind can look through the glass of the years.

He has sat in the stalls, opera-glass in hand; he has met women of thirty at balls, and has sat with them beneath shadowy curtains; he knows that the world is full of beautiful women, all waiting to be loved and amused, the circles of his immediate years are filled with feminine faces, they cluster like flowers on this side and that, and they fade into garden-like spaces of colour. How many may love him? The loveliest may one day smile upon his knee! and shall he renounce all for that little creature who has just finished singing and is handing round cups of tea? Every bachelor contemplating marriage says, "I shall have to give up all for one, one."

The young girl is often pretty but her prettiness is vague and uncertain, it inspires a sort of pitying admiration, but it suggests nothing; the very essence of the young girl's being is that she should have nothing to suggest, therefore the beauty of the young face fails to touch the imagination. No past lies hidden in those translucent eyes, no story of hate, disappointment, or sin. Nor is there in nine hundred and ninety-nine cases in a thousand any doubt that the hand, that spends at least a pound a day in restaurants and cabs, will succeed in gathering the muslin flower if he so wills it, and by doing so he will delight everyone. Where, then, is the struggle? where, then, is the triumph? Therefore, I say that if a young man's heart is not set on children, and tiresome dinner-parties, the young girl presents to him no possible ideal. But the woman of thirty presents from the outset all that is necessary to ensnare the heart of a young man. I see her sitting in her beautiful drawing-room, all designed by, and all belonging to her. Her chair is placed beneath an evergreen plant, and the long leaves lean out as if to touch her neck. The great white and red roses of the Aubusson carpet are spread enigmatically about her feline feet; a grand piano leans its melodious mouth to her; and there she sits when her visitors have left her, playing Beethoven's sonatas in the dreamy firelight. The spring-tide shows but a bloom of unvarying freshness; August has languished and loved in the strength of the sun. She is stately, she is tall. What sins, what disappointments, what aspirations lie in those grey eyes, mysteriously still, and mysteriously revealed. These a young man longs to know of, they are his life. He imagines himself sitting by her, when the others have gone, holding her hand, calling on her name; sometimes she moves away and plays the moonlight sonata. Letting her hands droop upon the keys she talks sadly, maybe affectionately; she speaks of the tedium of life, of its disenchantments. He knows well what she means, he has suffered as she has; but could he tell her, could she understand, that in his love reality would dissolve into a dream, all limitations would open into boundless infinity.

The husband he rarely sees. Sometimes a latch-key is heard about half-past six. The man is thick, strong, common, his jaws are heavy, his eyes are expressionless, there is about him the loud swagger of the *caserne*, and he suggests the inevitable question, Why did she marry him?—a question that every young man of refined mind asks a thousand times by day and ten thousand times by night, asks till he is five-and-thirty, and sees that his generation has passed into middle age.

Why did she marry him? Not the sea, nor the sky, nor the great mysterious midnight, when he opens his casement and gazes into starry space will give him answer; no Œdipus will ever come to unravel this riddle; this sphinx will never throw herself from the rock into the clangour of the sea-gulls and waves; she will never divulge her secret; and if she is the woman and not a woman of thirty, she has forgotten.

The young man shakes hands with the husband; he strives not to look embarrassed, and he talks of indifferent things—of how well he (the husband) is looking, of his amusements, his projects; and then he (the young man of refined mind) tastes of that keen and highly-seasoned delight—happiness in crime. He knows not the details of her home life, the husband is merely a dark cloud that fills one side of the picture, sometimes obliterating the sunlight; a shadowy shape that in certain moments solidifies and assumes the likeness of a rock-sculptured, imminent monster, but the shadow and the shape and the threat are magnetic, and in a sense of danger the fascination is sealed.

The young man of refined mind is in a ball-room! He leans against the woodwork in a distant doorway; hardly knowing what to do with himself, he strives to interest himself in the conversation of a group of men twice his age. I will not say he is shunned; but neither the matrons nor the young girls make any advances towards him. The young girls so sweet—in the oneness of their fresh hair, flowers, dresses, and glances—are being introduced, are getting up to dance, and the hostess is looking round for partners. She sees the young man in the doorway, but she hesitates and goes to someone else, and if you asked her why, she could not tell you why she avoided him. Presently the woman of thirty enters. She is in white satin and diamonds. She looks for him—a circular glance. Calm with possession she passes to a seat, extending her hand here and there. She dances the eighth, twelfth, and fifteenth waltz with him.

Will he induce her to visit his rooms? Will they be like Marshall's—strange debauches of colour and Turkish lamps—or mine, an old cabinet, a faded pastel which embalms the memory of a pastoral century, my taste; or will it be a library,—two leather library chairs, a large escritoire, etc.? Be this as it may, whether the apartments be the ruthless extravagance of artistic impulse, or the subdued taste of the student, she, the woman of thirty, shall be there by night and day: her statue is there, and even when she is sleeping safe in her husband's arms, with fevered brow, he, the young man of refined mind, alone and lonely shall kneel and adore her.

And should she *not* visit his rooms? If the complex and various accidents of existence should have ruled out her life virtuously; if the many inflections of sentiment have decided against this last consummation, then she will wax to the complete, the unfathomable temptress—the Lilith of old—she will never set him free, and in the end will be found about his heart "one single golden hair." She shall haunt his wife's face and words (should he seek to rid himself of her by marriage), a bitter sweet, a half-welcome enchantment; she shall consume and destroy the strength and spirit of his life, leaving it desolation, a barren landscape, burnt and faintly scented with the sea. Fame and wealth shall slip like sand from him. She may be set aside for the cadence of a rhyme, for the flowing line of a limb, but when the passion of art has raged itself out, she shall return to blight the peace of the worker.

A terrible malady is she, a malady the ancients knew of and called nympholepsy—a beautiful name evocative and symbolic of its ideal aspect, "the breasts of the nymphs in the brake." And the disease is not extinct in these modern days, nor will it ever be so long as men shall yearn for the unattainable; and the prosy bachelors who trail their ill-fated lives from their chambers to their clubs know their malady, and they call it—the woman of thirty.

VIII

A Japanese dressing-gown, the ideality of whose tissue delights me, some fresh honey and milk set by this couch hung with royal fringes; and having partaken of this odorous refreshment, I call to Jack, my great python crawling about after a two months' fast. I tie up a guinea-pig to the *tabouret*, pure Louis XV, the little beast struggles and squeaks, the snake, his black, bead-like eyes are fixed, how superb are the oscillations. . . now he strikes; and with what exquisite gourmandise he lubricates and swallows.

Marshall is at the organ in the hall, he is playing a Gregorian chant, that beautiful hymn, the "Vexilla Regis," by Saint Fortunatus, the great poet of the Middle Ages. And, having turned over the leaves of "Les Fêtes Galantes," I sit down to write.

My original intention was to write some thirty or forty stories varying from thirty to three hundred lines in length. The nature of these stories is easy to imagine: there was the youth who wandered by night into a witches' sabbath, and was disputed for by the witches, young and old. There was the light o' love who went into the desert to tempt the holy man; but he died as he yielded; his arms stiffened by some miracle, and she was unable to free herself; she died of starvation, as her bondage loosened in decay. I had increased my difficulties by adopting as part of my task the introduction of all sorts of elaborate, and in many cases extravagantly composed metres, and I had begun to feel that I was working in sand, I could make no progress, the house I was raising crumbled and fell away on every side. These stories had one merit: they were all, so far as I can remember, perfectly constructed. For the art of telling a story clearly and dramatically, *selon les procédés de M. Scribe*, I had thoroughly learnt from old M. Duval, the author of a hundred and sixty plays, written in collaboration with more than a hundred of the best writers of his day, including the master himself, Gautier. I frequently met M. Duval at breakfast at a neighbouring *café*, and our conversation turned on *l'exposition de la pièce, préparer la situation, nous aurons des larmes*, etc. One day, as I sat waiting for him, I took up the *Voltaire*. It contained an article by M. Zola. *Naturalisme, la vérité, la science*, were repeated some half-a-dozen times. Hardly able to believe my eyes, I read that you should write, with as little imagination as possible, that plot in a novel or in a play was illiterate and puerile, and that the art of M. Scribe was an art of strings and wires, etc. I rose up from breakfast, ordered my coffee, and stirred the sugar, a little dizzy, like one who has received a violent blow on the head.

Echo-augury! Words heard in an unexpected quarter, but applying marvellously well to the besetting difficulty of the moment. The reader who has followed me so far will remember the instant effect the word "Shelley" had upon me in childhood, and how it called into existence a train of feeling that illuminated the vicissitudes and passions of many years, until it was finally assimilated and became part of my being; the reader will also remember how the mere mention, at a certain moment, of the word "France" awoke a vital impulse, even a sense of final ordination, and how the irrevocable message was obeyed, and how it led to the creation of a mental existence.

And now for a third time I experienced the pain and joy of a sudden and inward light. Naturalism, truth, the new art, above all the phrase, "the new art," impressed me as with a sudden sense of light. I was dazzled, and I vaguely understood that my "Roses of Midnight" were sterile eccentricities, dead flowers that could not be galvanised into any semblance of life, passionless in all their passion.

I had read a few chapters of the "Assommoir," as it appeared in *La République des Lettres*; I had cried, "ridiculous, abominable," only because it is characteristic of me to instantly form an opinion and assume at once a violent attitude. But now I bought up the back numbers of the *Voltaire*, and I looked forward to the weekly exposition of the new faith with febrile eagerness. The great zeal with which the new master continued his propaganda, and the marvellous way in which subjects the most diverse, passing events, political, social, religious, were caught up and turned into arguments for, or proof of the truth of naturalism astonished me wholly. The idea of a new art based upon science, in opposition to the art of the old world that was based on imagination, an art that should explain all things and embrace modern life in its entirety, in its endless ramifications, be, as it were, a new creed in a new civilisation, filled me with wonder, and I stood dumb before the vastness of the conception, and the towering height of the ambition. In my fevered fancy I saw a new race of writers that would arise, and with the aid of the novel would continue to a more glorious and legitimate conclusion the work that the prophets had begun; and at each development of the theory of the new art and its universal applicability, my wonder increased and my admiration choked me. If anyone should be tempted to turn to the books themselves to seek an explanation of this wild ecstasy, he would find nothing—as well drink the dregs of yesterday's champagne. One is lying before me now, and as I glance through the pages listlessly I say, "Only the simple crude statements of a man of powerful mind, but singularly narrow vision."

Still, although eager and anxious for the fray, I did not see how I was to participate in it. I was not a novelist, not yet a dramatic author, and the possibility of a naturalistic poet seemed to me not a little doubtful. I had clearly understood that the lyrical quality was to be forever banished; there were to be no harps and lutes in our heaven, only drums; and the preservation of all the essentials of poetry, by the simple enumeration of the utensils to be found in a back kitchen, sounded, I could not help thinking (here it becomes necessary to whisper), not unlike rigmarole. I waited for the master to speak. He had declared that the Republic would fall if it did not become instantly naturalistic; he would not, he could not pass over in silence so important a branch of literature as poetry, no matter how contemptible he might think it. If he could find nothing to praise, he must at least condemn. At last the expected article came. It was all that could be desired by one in my fever of mind. Hugo's claims had been previously disproven, but now Banville and Gautier were declared to be warmed-up dishes of the ancient world; Baudelaire was a naturalist, but he had been spoilt by the romantic influence of his generation. *Cependant* there were indications of the naturalistic movement even in poetry. I trembled with excitement, I could not read fast enough. Coppée had striven to simplify language; he had versified the street cries, *Achetez la France, le Soir, le Rappel*; he had sought to give utterance to humble sentiments as in "Le Petit Epicier de Montrouge," the little grocer *qui cassait le sucre avec mélancolie*; Richepin had boldly and frankly adopted the language of the people in all its superb crudity. All this was, however, preparatory and tentative. We are waiting for our poet, he who will sing to us fearlessly of the rude industry of dustmen and the comestible glories of the market-places. The subjects are to hand, the formula alone is wanting.

The prospect dazzled me; I tried to calm myself. Had I the stuff in me to win and to wear these bays, this stupendous laurel crown?—bays, laurel crown, a distinct *souvenir* of Parnassus, but there is no modern equivalent, I must strive to invent a new one, in the meantime let me think. True it is that Swinburne was before me with the "Romantiques." The hymn to Proserpine and Dolores are wonderful lyrical versions of

Mdlle. de Maupin. In form the Leper is old English, the colouring is Baudelaire, but the rude industry of the dustmen and the comestible glories of the market-place shall be mine. *A bas "Les Roses de Minuit"*!

I felt the "naturalisation" of the "Roses of Midnight" would prove a difficult task. I soon found it an impossible one, and I laid the poems aside and commenced a volume redolent of the delights of Bougival and Ville d'Avray. This book was to be entitled "Poems of 'Flesh and Blood.'"

"*Elle mit son plus beau chapeau, son chapeau bleu*" . . . and then? Why, then picking up her skirt she threads her way through the crowded streets, reads the advertisements on the walls, hails the omnibus, inquires at the *concierge's* loge, murmurs as she goes upstairs, "*Que c'est haut le cinquième*," and then? Why, the door opens, and she cries, "*Je t'aime*"

But it was the idea of the new æstheticism—the new art corresponding to modern, as ancient art corresponded to ancient life—that captivated me, that led me away, and not a substantial knowledge of the work done by the naturalists. I had read the "Assommoir," and had been much impressed by its pyramid size, strength, height, and decorative grandeur, and also by the immense harmonic development of the idea; and the fugal treatment of the different scenes had seemed to me astonishingly new—the washhouse, for example: the fight motive is indicated, then follows the development of side issues, then comes the fight motive explained; it is broken off short, it flutters through a web of progressive detail, the fight motive is again taken up, and now it is worked out in all its fulness; it is worked up to *crescendo*, another side issue is introduced, and again the theme is given forth. And I marvelled greatly at the lordly, river-like roll of the narrative, sometimes widening out into lakes and shallowing meres, but never stagnating in fen or marshlands. The language, too, which I did not then recognise as the weak point, being little more than a boiling down of Chateaubriand and Flaubert, spiced with Goncourt, delighted me with its novelty, its richness, its force. Nor did I then even roughly suspect that the very qualities which set my admiration in a blaze wilder than wildfire, being precisely those that had won the victory for the romantic school forty years before, were very antagonistic to those claimed for the new art; I was deceived, as was all my generation, by a certain externality, an outer skin, a nearness, *un approchement*; in a word, by a substitution of Paris for the distant and exotic backgrounds so beloved of the romantic school. I did not know then, as I do now, that art is eternal, that it is only the artist that changes, and that the two great divisions—the only possible divisions—are: those who have talent, and those who have no talent. But I do not regret my errors, my follies; it is not well to know at once of the limitations of life and things. I should be less than nothing had it not been for my enthusiasms; they were the saving clause in my life.

But although I am apt to love too dearly the art of my day, and to the disparagement of that of other days, I did not fall into the fatal mistake of placing the realistic writers of 1877 side by side with and on the same plane of intellectual vision as the great Balzac; I felt that that vast immemorial mind rose above them all, like a mountain above the highest tower.

And, strange to say, it was Gautier that introduced me to Balzac; for mention is made in the wonderful preface to "Les Fleurs du Mal" of Seraphita: Seraphita, Seraphitus; which is it?—woman or man? Should Wilfred or Mona be the possessor? A new Mdlle. de Maupin, with royal lily and aureole, cloud-capped mountains, great gulfs of sea-water flowing up and reflecting as in a mirror the steep cliff's side; the straight white feet are set thereon, the obscuring weft of flesh is torn, and the pure, strange soul continues its mystical exhortations. Then the radiant vision, a white glory, the last outburst and manifestation, the trumpets of the apocalypse, the colour of heaven, the closing of this stupendous allegory—Seraphita lying dead in the rays of the first sun of the nineteenth century.

I, therefore, had begun, as it were, to read Balzac backwards; instead of beginning with the plain, simple, earthly tragedy of the Père Goriot, I first knelt in a beautiful but distant coigne of the great world of his genius—Seraphita. Certain *nuances* of soul are characteristic of certain latitudes, and what subtle instinct led him to Norway in quest of this fervent soul? The instincts of genius are unfathomable? but he who has known the white northern women with their pure spiritual eyes, will aver that instinct led him aright. I have known one, one whom I used to call Seraphita; Coppée knew her too, and that exquisite volume, "L'Exilé," so Seraphita-like in the keen blonde passion of its verse, was written to her, and each poem was sent to her as it was written. Where is she now, that flower of northern snow, once seen for a season in Paris? Has she returned to her native northern solitudes, great gulfs of sea water, mountain rock, and pine?

Balzac's genius is in his titles as heaven is in its stars: "Melmoth Reconcilié," "Jesus-Christ en Flandres," "Le Revers d'un Grand Homme,"

"La Cousine Bette." I read somewhere not very long ago, that Balzac was the greatest thinker that had appeared in France since Pascal. Of Pascal's claim to be a great thinker I confess I cannot judge. No man is greater than the age he lives in, and, therefore, to talk to us, the legitimate children of the nineteenth century, of logical proofs of the existence of God strikes us in just the same light as the logical proof of the existence of Jupiter Ammon. "Les Pensées" could appear to me only as infinitely childish; the form is no doubt superb, but tiresome and sterile to one of such modern and exotic taste as myself. Still, I accept thankfully, in its sense of two hundred years, the compliment paid to Balzac; but I would add that personally he seems to me to have shown greater wings of mind than any artist that ever lived. I am aware that this last statement will make many cry "fool" and hiss "Shakespeare"! But I am not putting forward these criticisms axiomatically, but only as the expressions of an individual taste, and interesting so far as they reveal to the reader the different developments and the progress of my mind. It might prove a little tiresome, but it would no doubt "look well," in the sense that going to church "looks well," if I were to write in here ten pages of praise of our national bard. I must, however, resist the temptation to "look well"; a confession is interesting in proportion to the amount of truth it contains, and I will, therefore, state frankly I never derived any profit whatsoever, and very little pleasure from the reading of the great plays. The beauty of the verse! Yes; he who loved Shelley so well as I could not fail to hear the melody of—

> *"Music to hear, why hearest thou music sadly?*
> *Sweets with sweets war not, joy delights in joy."*

Is not such music as this enough? Of course, but I am a sensualist in literature. I may see perfectly well that this or that book is a work of genius, but if it doesn't "fetch me," it doesn't concern me, and I forget its very existence. What leaves me cold today will madden me tomorrow. With me literature is a question of sense, intellectual sense if you will, but sense all the same, and ruled by the same caprices—those of the flesh? Now we enter on very subtle distinctions. No doubt that there is the brain-judgment and the sense-judgment of a work of art. And it will be noticed that these two forces of discrimination exist sometimes almost independently of each other, in rare and radiant instances confounded and blended in one immense and unique love. Who has not been, unless perhaps some dusty old pedant, thrilled and driven to pleasure by the action of a book that penetrates to and speaks to you of your most present and most intimate emotions. This is of course pure sensualism; but to take a less marked stage. Why should Marlowe enchant me? why should he delight and awake enthusiasm in me, while Shakespeare leaves me cold? The mind that can understand one can understand the other, but there are affinities in literature corresponding to, and very analogous to, sexual affinities—the same unreasoned attractions, the same pleasures, the same lassitudes. Those we have loved most we are most indifferent to. Shelley, Gautier, Zola, Flaubert, Goncourt! how I have loved you all; and now I could not, would not, read you again. How womanly, how capricious; but even a capricious woman is constant, if not faithful to her *amant de cœur*. And so with me; of those I have loved deeply there is but one that still may thrill me with the old passion, with the first ecstasy—it is Balzac. Upon that rock I built my church, and his great and valid talent saved me often from destruction, saved me from the shoaling waters of new æstheticisms, the putrid mud of naturalism, and the faint and sickly surf of the symbolists. Thinking of him, I could not forget that it is the spirit and not the flesh that is eternal; that, as it was thought that in the first instance gave man speech, so to the end it shall still be thought that shall make speech beautiful and rememberable. The grandeur and sublimity of Balzac's thoughts seem to me to rise to the loftiest heights, and his range is limitless; there is no passion he has not touched, and what is more marvellous, he has given to each in art a place equivalent to the place it occupies in nature; his intense and penetrating sympathy for human life and all that concerns it enabled him to surround the humblest subjects with awe and crown them with the light of tragedy. There are some, particularly those who can understand neither and can read but one, who will object to any comparison being drawn between the Dramatist and the Novelist; but I confess that I—if the inherent superiority of verse over prose, which I admit unhesitatingly, be waived—that I fail, utterly fail to see in what Shakespeare is greater than Balzac. The range of the poet's thought is of necessity not so wide, and his concessions must needs be greater than the novelist's. On these points we will cry quits, and come at once to the vital question—the creation. Is Lucien inferior to Hamlet? Is Eugénie Grandet inferior to Desdemona? Is her father inferior to Shylock? Is Macbeth inferior to Vautrin? Can it be said that the apothecary in the "Cousine Bette," or the Baron Hulot, or the Cousine Bette herself is inferior to anything the brain of man has ever conceived? And it must not be forgotten that Shakespeare has had three hundred years and the advantage of stage representation to impress his characters on the sluggish mind of the world; and as mental impressions are governed by the same laws of gravitation as atoms, our realisation of Falstaff must of necessity be more vivid than any character in contemporary literature, although it were equally great. And so far as epigram and aphorism are concerned, and here I speak with absolute sincerity and conviction, the work of the novelist seems to me richer than that of the dramatist. Who shall forget those terrible words of the poor life-weary orphan in the boarding-house? Speaking of Vautrin she says, "His look frightens me as if he put his hand on my dress"; and another epigram from the same book, "Woman's virtue is man's greatest invention." Find me anything in La Rochefoucauld that goes more incisively to the truth of things. One more; here I can give the exact words: "*La gloire est le soleil des morts.*" It would be easy to compile a book of sayings from Balzac that would make all "Maximes" and "Pensées," even those of La Rochefoucauld or Joubert, seem trivial and shallow.

Balzac was the great moral influence of my life, and my reading culminated in the "Comédie Humaine." I no doubt fluttered through some scores of other books, of prose and verse, sipping a little honey, but he alone left any important or lasting impression upon my mind. The rest was like walnuts and wine, an agreeable aftertaste.

But notwithstanding all this reading I can lay no claim to scholarship of any kind; for save life I could never learn anything correctly. I am a student only of ball rooms, bar rooms, streets, and alcoves. I have read very little; but all I read I can turn to account, and all I read I remember. To read freely, extensively, has always been my ambition, and my utter inability to study has always been to me a subject of grave inquietude,— study as contrasted with a general and haphazard gathering of ideas taken in flight. But in me the impulse is so original to frequent the haunts of men that it is irresistible, conversation is the breath of my nostrils, I watch the movement of life, and my ideas spring from it uncalled for, as buds from branches. Contact with the world is in me the generating force; without this what invention I have is thin and sterile, and it grows thinner rapidly, until it dies away utterly, as it did in the composition of my unfortunate "Roses of Midnight."

Men and women, oh the strength of the living faces! conversation, oh the magic of it! It is a fabulous river of gold where the precious metal is washed up without stint for all to take, to take as much as he can carry. Two old ladies discussing the peerage? Much may be learned, it is gold; poets and wits, then it is fountains whose spray solidifies into jewels, and every herb and plant is begemmed with the sparkle of the diamond and the glow of the ruby.

I did not go to either Oxford or Cambridge, but I went to the "Nouvelle Athènes." What is the "Nouvelle Athènes"? He who would know anything of my life must know something of the academy of the fine arts. Not the official stupidity you read of in the daily papers, but the real French academy, the *café*. The "Nouvelle Athènes" is a *café* on the Place Pigale. Ah! the morning idlenesses and the long evenings when life was but a summer illusion, the grey moonlights on the Place where we used to stand on the pavements, the shutters clanging up behind us, loath to separate, thinking of what we had left said, and how much better we might have enforced our arguments. Dead and scattered are all those who used to assemble there, and those years and our home, for it was our home, live only in a few pictures and a few pages of prose. The same old story, the vanquished only are victorious; and though unacknowledged, though unknown, the influence of the "Nouvelle Athènes" is inveterate in the artistic thought of the nineteenth century.

How magnetic, intense, and vivid are these memories of youth. With what strange, almost unnatural clearness do I see and hear,—see the white face of that *café*, the white nose of that block of houses, stretching up to the Place, between two streets. I can see down the incline of those two streets, and I know what shops are there; I can hear the glass door of the *café* grate on the sand as I open it. I can recall the smell of every hour. In the morning that of eggs frizzling in butter, the pungent cigarette, coffee and bad cognac; at five o'clock the fragrant odour of absinthe; and soon after the steaming soup ascends from the kitchen; and as the evening advances, the mingled smells of cigarettes, coffee, and weak beer. A partition, rising a few feet or more over the hats, separates the glass front from the main body of the *café*. The usual marble tables are there, and it is there we sat and æstheticised till two o'clock in the morning. But who is that man? he whose prominent eyes flash with excitement. That is Villiers de l'Isle-Adam. The last or the supposed last of the great family. He is telling that girl a story—that fair girl with heavy eyelids, stupid and sensual. She is, however, genuinely astonished and interested, and he is striving to play upon her ignorance. Listen to him. "Spain—the night is fragrant with the sea and the perfume of the orange trees, you know—a midnight of stars and dreams. Now and then the silence is broken by the sentries challenging—that is all. But not in Spanish but in French are the challenges given; the town is in the hands of the French; it is under martial law. But now an officer passes down a certain garden, a Spaniard disguised as a French officer; from the balcony the family—one of the most noble and oldest families Spain can boast of, a thousand years, long before the conquest of the Moors—watches him. Well then"—Villiers sweeps with a white feminine hand the long hair that is falling over his face—he has half forgotten, he is a little mixed in the opening of the story, and he is striving in English to "scamp," in French to *escamoter*. "The family are watching, death if he is caught, if he fails to kill the French sentry. The cry of a bird, some vague sound attracts the sentry, he turns; all is lost. The Spaniard is seized. Martial law, Spanish conspiracy must be put down. The French general is a man of iron." (Villiers laughs, a short, hesitating laugh that is characteristic of him, and continues in his abrupt, uncertain way), "man of iron; not only he declares that the spy must be beheaded, but also the entire family—a man of iron that, ha, ha; and then, no you cannot, it is impossible for you to understand the enormity of the calamity—a thousand years before the conquest by the Moors, a Spaniard alone could—there is no one here, ha, ha, I was forgetting—the utter extinction of a great family of the name, the oldest and noblest of all the families in Spain, it is not easy to understand that, no, not easy here in the 'Nouvelle Athènes'—ha, ha, one must belong to a great family to understand, ha, ha.

"The father beseeches, he begs that one member may be spared to continue the name—the youngest son—that is all; if he could be saved, the rest what matter; death is nothing to a Spaniard; the family, the name, a thousand years of name is everything. The general is, you know, a 'man of iron.' 'Yes, one member of your family shall be respited, but on one condition.' To the agonised family conditions are as nothing. But they don't know the man of iron is determined to make a terrible example, and they cry, 'Any conditions.' 'He who is respited must serve as executioner to the others.' Great is the doom; you understand; but after all the name must be saved. Then in the family council the father goes to his youngest son and says, 'I have been a good father to you, my son; I have always been a kind father, have I not? answer me; I have never refused you anything. Now you will not fail us, you will prove yourself worthy of the great name you bear. Remember your great ancestor who defeated the Moors, remember.'" (Villiers strives to get in a little local colour, but his knowledge of Spanish names and history is limited, and he in a certain sense fails.) "Then the mother comes to her son and says, 'My son, I have been a good mother, I have always loved you; say you will not desert us in this hour of our great need.' Then the little sister comes, and the whole family kneels down and appeals to the horror-stricken boy. . .

"'He will not prove himself unworthy of our name,' cries the father. 'Now, my son, courage, take the axe firmly, do what I ask you, courage, strike straight.' The father's head falls into the sawdust, the blood all over the white beard; then comes the elder brother, and then another brother; and then, oh, the little sister was almost more than he could bear, and the mother had to whisper, 'Remember your promise to your father, to your dead father.' The mother laid her head on the block, but he could not strike. 'Be not the first coward of our name, strike; remember your promise to us all,' and her head was struck off."

"And the son," the girl asks, "what became of him?"

"He never was seen, save at night, walking, a solitary man, beneath the walls of his castle in Granada."

"And whom did he marry?"

"He never married."

Then after a long silence someone said,—

"Whose story is that?"

"Balzac's."

At that moment the glass door of the *café* grated upon the sanded floor, and Manet entered. Although by birth and by art essentially Parisian, there was something in his appearance and manner of speaking that often suggested an Englishman. Perhaps it was his dress—his clean-cut clothes and figure. That figure! those square shoulders that swaggered as he went across a room and the thin waist; and that face, the beard and nose, satyr-like shall I say? No, for I would evoke an idea of beauty of line united to that of intellectual expression—frank words, frank passion in his convictions, loyal and simple phrases, clear as well-water, sometimes a little hard, sometimes, as they flowed away, bitter, but at the fountain head sweet and full of light. He sits next to Degas, that round-shouldered man in suit of pepper and salt. There is nothing very trenchantly French about him either, except the large necktie; his eyes are small and his words are sharp, ironical, cynical. These two men are the leaders of the impressionist school. Their friendship has been jarred by inevitable rivalry. "Degas was painting 'Semiramis' when I was painting 'Modern Paris,'" says Manet. "Manet is in despair because he cannot paint atrocious pictures like Durant, and be fêted and decorated; he is an artist, not by inclination, but by force. He is as a galley slave chained to the oar," says Degas. Different too are their methods of work. Manet paints his whole picture from nature, trusting his instinct to lead him aright through the devious labyrinth of selection. Nor does his instinct ever fail him, there is a vision in his eyes which he calls nature, and which he paints unconsciously as he digests his food, thinking and declaring vehemently that the artist should not seek a synthesis, but should paint merely what he sees. This extraordinary oneness of nature and artistic vision does not exist in Degas, and even his portraits are composed from drawings and notes. About midnight Catulle Mendès will drop in, when he has corrected his proofs. He will come with his fine paradoxes and his strained eloquence. He will lean towards you, he will take you by the arm, and his presence is a nervous pleasure. And when the *café* is closed, when the last bock has been drunk, we shall walk about the great moonlight of the Place Pigale, and through the dark shadows of the streets, talking of the last book published, he hanging on to my arm, speaking in that high febrile voice of his, every phrase luminous, aerial, even as the soaring moon and the fitful clouds. Duranty, an unknown Stendhal, will come in for an hour or so; he will talk little and go away quietly; he knows, and his whole manner shows that he knows that he is a defeated man; and if you ask him why he does not write another novel, he will say, "What's the good, it would not be read; no one read the others, and I mightn't do even as well if I tried again." Paul Alexis, Léon Diex, Pissarro, Cabaner, are also frequently seen in the "Nouvelle Athènes."

Cabaner! the world knows not the names of those who scorn the world: somewhere in one of the great populous churchyards of Paris there is a forgotten grave, and there lies Cabaner. Cabaner! since the beginning there have been, till the end of time there shall be Cabaners; and they shall live miserably and they shall die miserable, and shall be forgotten; and there shall never arise a novelist great enough to make live in art that eternal spirit of devotion, disinterestedness, and aspiration, which in each generation incarnates itself in one heroic soul. Better wast thou than those who stepped to opulence and fame upon thee fallen; better, loftier-minded, purer; thy destiny was to fall that others might rise upon thee, thou wert one of the noble legion of the conquered; let praise be given to the conquered, for with them lies the brunt of victory. Child of the pavement, of strange sonnets and stranger music, I remember thee; I remember the silk shirts, the four sous of Italian cheese, the roll of bread, and the glass of milk, the streets were thy dining-room. And the five-mile walk daily to the suburban music hall where five francs were earned by playing the accompaniments of comic songs. And the wonderful room on the fifth floor, which was furnished when that celebrated heritage of two thousand francs was paid. I remember the fountain that was bought for a wardrobe, and the American organ with all the instruments of the orchestra, and the plaster casts under which the homeless ones that were never denied a refuge and a crust by thee slept. I remember all, and the buying of the life-size "Venus de Milo." Something extraordinary would be done with it, I knew, but the result exceeded my wildest expectation. The head must needs be struck off, so that the rapture of thy admiration should be secure from all jarring reminiscence of the streets.

Then the wonderful story of the tenor, the pork butcher, who was heard giving out such a volume of sound that the sausages were set in motion above him; he was fed, clothed, and educated on the five francs a day earned in the music hall in the Avenue de la Motte Piquet; and when he made his *début* at the Théâtre Lyrique, thou wast in the last stage of consumption and too ill to go to hear thy pupil's success. He was immediately engaged by Mapleson and taken to America.

I remember thy face, Cabaner; I can see it now—that long sallow face ending in a brown beard, and the hollow eyes, the meagre arms covered with a silk shirt, contrasting strangely with the rest of the dress. In all thy privation and poverty, thou didst never forego thy silk shirt. I remember the paradoxes and the aphorisms, if not the exact words, the glamour and the sentiment of a humour that was all thy own. Never didst thou laugh; no, not even when in discussing how silence might be rendered in music, thou didst say, with thy extraordinary Pyrenean accent, "*Pour rendre le silence en musique il me faudrait trois orchestres militaires.*" And when I did show thee some poor verses of mine, French verses, for at this time I hated and had partly forgotten my native language—

"My dear George Moore, you always write about love, the subject is nauseating."

"So it is, so it is; but after all Baudelaire wrote about love and lovers; his best poem. . ."

"*C'est vrai, mais il s'agissait d'une charogne et cela relève beaucoup la chose.*"

I remember, too, a few stray snatches of thy extraordinary music, "music that might be considered by Wagner as a little too advanced, but which Liszt would not fail to understand"; also thy settings of sonnets where the *melody* was continued uninterruptedly from the first line to the last; and that still more marvellous feat, thy setting, likewise with unbroken melody, of Villon's ballade "Les Dames du Temps Jadis"; and that Out-Cabanering of Cabaner, the putting to music of Cros's "Hareng Saur."

And why didst thou remain ever poor and unknown? Because of something too much, or something too little? Because of something too much! so I think, at least; thy heart was too full of too pure an ideal, too far removed from all possible contagion with the base crowd.

But, Cabaner, thou didst not labour in vain; thy destiny, though obscure, was a valiant and fruitful one; and, as in life, thou didst live for others so now in death thou dost live in others, Thou wast in an hour of wonder and strange splendour when the last tints and lovelinesses of romance lingered in the deepening west; when out of the clear east rose with a mighty effulgence of colour and lawless light Realism; when showing aloft in the dead pallor of the zenith, like a white flag fluttering faintly, Symbolists and Decadents appeared. Never before was there so sudden a flux and conflux of artistic desire, such aspiration in the soul of man, such rage of passion, such fainting fever, such cerebral erethism. The roar and dust of the daily battle of the Realists was continued under the flush of the sunset, the arms of the Romantics glittered, the pale spiritual Symbolists watched and waited, none knowing yet of their presence. In such an hour of artistic convulsion and renewal of thought thou wast, and thou wast a magnificent rallying point for all comers; it was thou who didst theorise our confused aspirations, and by thy holy example didst save us from all base commercialism, from all hateful prostitution; thou wast ever our high priest, and from thy high altar turned to us the white host, the ideal, the true and living God of all men.

Cabaner, I see you now entering the "Nouvelle Athènes"; you are a little tired after your long weary walk, but you lament not and you never cry out against the public that will accept neither your music nor your poetry. But though you are tired and footsore, you are ready to æstheticise till the *café* closes; for you the homeless ones are waiting:

there they are, some three or four, and you will take them to your strange room, furnished with the American organ, the fountain, and the decapitated Venus, and you will give them a crust each and cover them with what clothes you have; and, when clothes are lacking, with plaster casts, and though you will take but a glass of milk yourself, you will find a few sous to give them *lager* to cool their thirsty throats. So you have ever lived—a blameless life is yours, no base thought has ever entered there, not even a woman's love; art and friends, that is all.

Reader, do you know of anything more angelic? If you do you are more fortunate than I have been.

IX

The Synthesis of the Nouvelle Athenes

Two dominant notes in my character—an original hatred of my native country, and a brutal loathing of the religion I was brought up in. All the aspects of my native country are violently disagreeable to me, and I cannot think of the place I was born in without a sensation akin to nausea. These feelings are inherent and inveterate in me. I am instinctively averse from my own countrymen; they are at once remote and repulsive; but with Frenchmen I am conscious of a sense of nearness; I am one with them in their ideas and aspirations, and when I am with them, I am alive with a keen and penetrating sense of intimacy. Shall I explain this by atavism? Was there a French man or woman in my family some half-dozen generations ago? I have not inquired. The English I love, and with a love that is foolish—mad, limitless; I love them better than the French, but I am not so near to them. Dear, sweet Protestant England, the red tiles of the farmhouse, the elms, the great hedgerows, and all the rich fields adorned with spreading trees, and the weald and the wold, the very words are passionately beautiful southern England, not the north,—there is something Celtic in the north—southern England, with its quiet, steadfast faces—a smock frock is to me one of the most delightful things in the world; it is so absolutely English. The villages clustered round the greens, the spires of the churches pointing between the elm trees. . . This is congenial to me; and this is Protestantism. England is Protestantism, Protestantism is England. Protestantism is strong, clean, and westernly, Catholicism is eunuch-like, dirty, and Oriental. . . There is something even Chinese about it. What made England great was Protestantism, and when she ceases to be Protestant she will fall. . . Look at the nations that have clung to Catholicism, starving moonlighters and starving brigands. The Protestant flag floats on every ocean breeze, the Catholic banner hangs limp in the incense silence of the Vatican. Let us be Protestant, and revere Cromwell.

Garçon, un bock! I write to please myself, just as I order my dinner; if my books sell I cannot help it—it is an accident.

But you live by writing.

Yes, but life is only an accident—art is eternal.

What I reproach Zola with is that he has no style; there is nothing you won't find in Zola from Chateaubriand to the reporting in the *Figaro*.

He seeks immortality in an exact description of a linendraper's shop; if the shop conferred immortality it should be upon the linendraper who created the shop, and not on the novelist who described it.

And his last novel "l'Œuvre," how spun out, and for a franc a line in the "Gil Blas." Not a single new or even exact observation. And that terrible phrase repeated over and over again—"La Conquête de Paris." What does it mean? I never knew anyone who thought of conquering Paris; no one ever spoke of conquering Paris except, perhaps, two or three provincials.

You must have rules in poetry, if it is only for the pleasure of breaking them, just as you must have women dressed, if it is only for the pleasure of undressing them.

FANCY, A BANQUET WAS GIVEN to Julien by his pupils! He made a speech in favour of Lefebvre, and hoped that everyone there would vote for Lefebvre. Julien was very eloquent. He spoke of *Le grand art, le nu*, and Lefebvre's unswerving fidelity to *le nu* . . . elegance, refinement, an echo of ancient Greece: and then,—what do you think? when he had exhausted all the reasons why the medal of honour should be accorded to Lefebvre, he said, "I ask you to remember, gentlemen, that he has a wife and eight children." Is it not monstrous?

But it is you who are monstrous, you who expect to fashion the whole world in conformity with your æstheticisms. . . a vain dream, and if realised it would result in an impossible world. A wife and children are the basis of existence, and it is folly to cry out because an appeal to such interests as these meet with response. . . it will be so till the end of time.

And these great interests that are to continue to the end of time began two years ago, when your pictures were not praised in the *Figaro* as much as you thought they should be.

Love—but not marriage. Marriage means a four-post bed and papa and mamma between eleven and twelve. Love is aspiration: transparencies, colour, light, a sense of the unreal. But a wife—you know all about her—who her father was, who her mother was, what she thinks of you and her opinion of the neighbours over the way.

Where, then, is the dream, the *au delà*? But the women one has never seen before, that one will never see again! The choice! the enervation of burning odours, the baptismal whiteness of women, light, ideal tissues, eyes strangely dark with kohl, names that evoke palm trees and ruins, Spanish moonlight or maybe Persepolis! The nightingale-harmony of an eternal yes—the whisper of a sweet unending yes. The unknown, the unreal. This is love. There is delusion, an *au delà*.

Good heavens! and the world still believes in education, in teaching people the "grammar of art." Education should be confined to clerks, and it drives even them to drink. Will the world learn that we never learn anything that we did not know before? The artist, the poet, painter, musician, and novelist go straight to the food they want, guided by an unerring and ineffable instinct; to teach them is to destroy the nerve of the artistic instinct. Art flees before the art school. . . "correct drawing," "solid painting." Is it impossible to teach people, to force it into their heads that there is no such thing as correct drawing, and that if drawing were correct it would be wrong? Solid painting; good heavens! Do they suppose that there is one sort of painting that is better than all others, and that there is a receipt for making it as for making chocolate! Art is not mathematics, it is individuality. It does not matter how badly you paint, so long as you don't paint badly like other people. Education destroys individuality. That great studio of Julien's is a sphinx, and all the poor folk that go there for artistic education are devoured. After two years they all paint and draw alike, everyone; that vile execution,— they call it execution,—*la pâte, la peinture au premier coup*. I was over in England last year, and I saw some portraits by a man called Richmond. They were horrible, but I liked them because they weren't like painting. Stott and Sargent are clever fellows enough; I like Stott the best. If they had remained at home and hadn't been taught, they might have developed a personal art, but the trail of the serpent is over all they do—that vile French painting, *le morceau*, etc. Stott is getting over it by degrees. He exhibited a nymph this year. I know what he meant; it was an interesting intention. I liked his little landscapes better. . . simplified into nothing, into a couple of primitive tints, wonderful clearness, light. But I doubt if he will find a public to understand all that.

Democratic art! Art is the direct antithesis to democracy. . . Athens! a few thousand citizens who owned many thousand slaves, call that democracy! No! what I am speaking of is modern democracy—the mass. The mass can only appreciate simple and *naïve* emotions, puerile prettiness, above all conventionalities. See the Americans that come over here; what do they admire? Is it Degas or Manet they admire? No, Bouguereau and Lefebvre. What was most admired at the International Exhibition?—The Dirty Boy. And if the medal of honour had been decided by a *plébiscite*, the dirty boy would have had an overwhelming majority. What is the literature of the people? The idiotic stories of the *Petit Journal*. Don't talk of Shakespeare, Molière and the masters; they are accepted on the authority of the centuries. If the people could understand *Hamlet*, the people would not read the *Petit Journal*; if the people could understand Michel Angelo, they would not look at our Bouguereau or your Bouguereau, Sir F. Leighton. For the last hundred years we have been going rapidly towards democracy, and what is the result? The destruction of the handicrafts. That there are still good pictures painted and good poems written proves nothing, there will always be found men to sacrifice their lives for a picture or a poem. But the decorative arts which are executed in collaboration, and depend for support on the general taste of a large number, have ceased to exist. Explain that if you can. I'll give you five thousand, ten thousand francs to buy a beautiful clock that is not a copy and is not ancient, and you can't do it. Such a thing does not exist. Look here, I was going up the staircase of the Louvre the other day. They were putting up a mosaic; it was horrible; everyone knows it is horrible. Well, I asked who had given the order for this mosaic, and I could not find out; no one knew. An order is passed from bureau to bureau, and no one is responsible; and it will be always so in a republic, and the more republican you are the worse it will be.

The world is dying of machinery; that is the great disease, that is the plague that will sweep away and destroy civilisation; man will have to rise against it sooner or later. . . Capital, unpaid labour, wage-slaves, and all the rest—stuff. . . Look at these plates; they were painted by machinery; they are abominable. Look at them. In old times plates were painted by the hand, and the supply was necessarily limited to the demand, and a china in which there was always something more or less pretty, was turned out; but now thousands, millions of plates are made more than we want, and there is a commercial crisis; the thing is inevitable. I say the great and the reasonable revolution will be when mankind rises in revolt, and smashes the machinery and restores the handicrafts.

Goncourt is not an artist, notwithstanding all his affectation and outcries; he is not an artist. *Il me fait l'effet* of an old woman shrieking after immortality and striving to beat down some fragment of it with a broom. Once it was a duet, now it is a solo. They wrote novels, history, plays, they collected *bric-à-brac*—they wrote about their *bric-à-brac*; they painted in water-colours, they etched—they wrote about their water-colours and etchings; they have made a will settling that the *bric-à-brac* is to be sold at their death, and the proceeds applied to founding a prize for the best essay or novel, I forget which it is. They wrote about the prize they are going to found; they kept a diary, they wrote down everything they heard, felt, or saw, *radotage de vieille femme*; nothing must escape, not the slightest word; it might be that very word that might confer on them immortality; everything they heard, or said, must be of value, of inestimable value. A real artist does not trouble himself about immortality, about everything he hears, feels and says; he treats ideas and sensations as so much clay wherewith to create.

And then the famous collaboration; how it was talked about, written about, prayed about; and when Jules died, what a subject for talk for articles; it all went into pot. Hugo's vanity was Titanic, Goncourt's is puerile.

And Daudet?

Oh, Daudet, *c'est de la bouillabaisse*.

Whistler, of all artists, is the least impressionist; the idea people have of his being an impressionist only proves once again the absolute inability of the public to understand the merits or the demerits of artistic work. Whistler's art is classical; he thinks of nature, but he does not see nature; he is guided by his mind, and not by his eyes; and the best of it is he says so. He knows it well enough! Anyone who knows him must have heard him say, "Painting is absolutely scientific; it is an exact science." And his work is in accord with his theory; he risks nothing, all is brought down, arranged, balanced, and made one; his pictures are thought out beforehand, they are mental conceptions. I admire his work; I am showing how he is misunderstood, even by those who think they understand. Does he ever seek a pose that is characteristic of the model, a pose that the model repeats oftener than any other?—Never. He advances the foot, puts the hand on the hip, etc., with a view to rendering his *idea*. Take his portrait of Duret. Did he ever see Duret in dress clothes? Probably not. Did he ever see Duret with a lady's opera cloak?—I am sure he never did. Is Duret in the habit of going to the theatre with ladies? No, he is a *littérateur* who is always in men's society, rarely in ladies'. But these facts mattered nothing to Whistler as they matter to Degas, or to Manet. Whistler took Duret out of his environment, dressed him up, thought out a scheme—in a word, painted his idea without concerning himself in the least with the model. Mark you, I deny that I am urging any fault or flaw; I am merely contending that Whistler's art is not modern art, but classic art—yes, and severely classical, far more classical than Titian's or Velasquez;—from an opposite pole as classical as Ingres. No Greek dramatist ever sought the synthesis of things more uncompromisingly than Whistler. And he is right. Art is not nature. Art is nature digested. Zola and Goncourt cannot, or will not understand that the artistic stomach must be allowed to do its work in its own mysterious fashion. If a man is really an artist he will remember what is necessary, forget what is useless; but if he takes notes he will interrupt his artistic digestion, and the result will be a lot of little touches, inchoate and wanting in the elegant rhythm of the synthesis.

I am sick of synthetical art; we want observation direct and unreasoned. What I reproach Millet with is that it is always the same thing, the same peasant, the same *sabot*, the same sentiment. You must admit that it is somewhat stereotyped.

What does that matter; what is more stereotyped than Japanese art? But that does not prevent it from being always beautiful.

People talk of Manet's originality; that is just what I can't see. What he has got, and what you can't take away from him, is a magnificent execution. A piece of still life by Manet is the most wonderful thing in the world; vividness of colour, breadth, simplicity, and directness of touch—marvellous!

French translation is the only translation; in England you still continue to translate poetry into poetry, instead of into prose. We used to do the same, but we have long ago renounced such follies. Either of two things—if the translator is a good poet, he substitutes his verse for that of the original;—I don't want his verse, I want the original;—if he is a bad poet; he gives us bad verse, which is intolerable. Where the original poet put an effect of cæsura, the translator puts an effect of rhyme; where the original poet puts an effect of rhyme, the translator puts an effect of cæsura. Take Longfellow's "Dante." Does it give as good an idea of the original as our prose translation? Is it as interesting reading? Take Bayard Taylor's translation of "Goethe." Is it readable? Not to anyone with an ear for verse. Will anyone say that Taylor's would be read if the original did not exist? The fragment translated by Shelley is beautiful, but then it is Shelley. Look at Swinburne's translations of Villon. They are beautiful poems by Swinburne, that is all; he makes Villon speak of a "splendid kissing mouth." Villon could not have done this unless he had read Swinburne. "Heine," translated by James Thomson, is not different from Thomson's original poems; "Heine," translated by Sir Theodore Martin, is doggerel.

But in English blank verse you can translate quite as literally as you could into prose?

I doubt it, but even so, the rhythm of the blank line would carry your mind away from that of the original.

But if you don't know the original? The rhythm of the original can be suggested in prose judiciously used; even if it isn't, your mind is at least free, whereas the English rhythm must destroy the sensation of something foreign. There is no translation except a word-for-word translation. Baudelaire's translation of Poe, and Hugo's translation of Shakespeare, are marvellous in this respect; a pun or joke that is untranslatable is explained in a note.

But that is the way young ladies translate—word for word!

No; 'tis just what they don't do; they think they are translating word for word, but they aren't. All the proper names, no matter how unpronounceable, must be rigidly adhered to; you must never transpose versts into kilometres, or roubles into francs;—I don't know what a verst is or what a rouble is, but when I see the words I am in Russia. Every proverb must be rendered literally, even if it doesn't make very good sense: if it doesn't make sense at all, it must be explained in a note. For example, there is a proverb in German: "*Quand le cheval est sellé il faut le monter*"; in French there is a proverb: "*Quand le vin est tiré il faut le boire*." Well, a translator who would translate *quand le cheval*, etc., by *quand le vin*, etc., is an ass, and does not know his business. In translation only a strictly classical language should be used; no word of slang, or even word of modern origin should be employed; the translator's aim should be never to dissipate the illusion of an exotic. If I were translating the "Assommoir" into English, I should strive after a strong, flexible, but colourless language, something—what shall I say?—the style of a modern Addison.

WHAT, DON'T YOU KNOW THE story about Mendès?—when *Chose* wanted to marry his sister? *Chose's* mother, it appears, went to live with a priest. The poor fellow was dreadfully cut up; he was broken-hearted; and he went to Mendès, his heart swollen with grief, determined to make a clean breast of it, let the worst come to the worst. After a great deal of beating about the bush, and apologising, he got it out. You know Mendès, you can see him smiling a little; and looking at *Chose* with that white cameo face of his he said,

"Avec quel meillur homme voulez-vous que votre mère se mit? vous n'avez donc, jeune homme, aucun sentiment religieux."

Victor Hugo, he is a painter on porcelain; his verse is mere decoration, long tendrils and flowers; and the same thing over and over again.

How to be happy!—not to read Baudelaire and Verlaine, not to enter the *Nouvelle Athènes*, unless perhaps to play dominoes like the *bourgeois* over there, not to do anything that would awake a too intense consciousness of life,—to live in a sleepy country side, to have a garden to work in, to have a wife and children, to chatter quietly every evening over the details of existence. We must have the azaleas out tomorrow and thoroughly cleansed, they are devoured by insects; the tame rook has flown away; mother lost her prayer-book coming from church, she thinks it was stolen. A good, honest, well-to-do peasant, who knows nothing of politics, must be very nearly happy;—and to think there are people who would educate, who would draw these people out of the calm satisfaction of their instincts, and give them passions! The philanthropist is the Nero of modern times.

X

Extract From a Letter

Why did you not send a letter? We have all been writing to you for the last six months, but no answer—none. Had you written one word I would have saved all. The poor *concierge* was in despair; she said the *propriétaire* would wait if you had only said when you were coming back, or if you only had let us know what you wished to be done. Three quarters rent was due, and no news could be obtained of you, so an auction had to be called. It nearly broke my heart to see those horrid men tramping over the delicate carpets, their coarse faces set against the sweet colour of that beautiful English cretonne. . . And all the while the pastel by Manet, the great hat set like an aureole about the face—'the eyes deep set in crimson shadow,' 'the fan widespread across the bosom' (you see I am quoting your own words), looking down, the mistress of that little paradise of tapestry. She seemed to resent the intrusion. I looked once or twice half expecting those eyes 'deep set in crimson shadow' to fill with tears. But nothing altered her great dignity; she seemed to see all, but as a Buddha she remained impenetrable. . .

"I was there the night before the sale. I looked through the books, taking notes of those I intended to buy—those which we used to read together when the snow lay high about the legs of the poor faun in *terre cuite*, that laughed amid the frosty *boulingrins*. I found a large packet of letters which I instantly destroyed. You should not be so careless; I wonder how it is that men are always careless about their letters.

"The sale was announced for one o'clock. I wore a thick veil, for I did not wish to be recognised; the *concierge* of course knew me, but she can be depended upon. The poor old woman was in tears, so sorry was she to see all your pretty things sold up. You left owing her a hundred francs, but I have paid her; and talking of you we waited till the auctioneer arrived. Everything had been pulled down; the tapestry from the walls, the picture, the two vases I gave you were on the table waiting the stroke of the hammer. And then the men, all the *marchands de meubles* in the *quartier*, came upstairs, spitting and talking coarsely—their foul voices went through me. They stamped, spat, pulled the things about, nothing escaped them. One of them held up the Japanese dressing-gown and made some horrible jokes; and the auctioneer, who was a humorist, answered, 'If there are any ladies' men present, we shall have some spirited bidding.' The pastel I bought, and I shall keep it and try to find some excuse to satisfy my husband, but I send you the miniature, and I hope you will not let it be sold again. There were many other things I should have liked to buy, but I did not dare—the organ that you used to play hymns on and I waltzes on, the Turkish lamp which we could never agree about. . . but when I saw the satin shoes which I gave you to carry the night of that adorable ball, and which you would not give back, but nailed up on the wall on either side of your bed and put matches in, I was seized with an almost invincible desire to steal them. I don't know why, *un caprice de femme*. No one but you would have ever thought of converting satin shoes into match boxes. I wore them at that delicious ball; we danced all night together, and you had an explanation with my husband (I was a little afraid for a moment, but it came out all right), and we went and sat on the balcony in the soft warm moonlight; we watched the glitter of epaulets and gas, the satin of the bodices, the whiteness of passing shoulders: we dreamed the massy darknesses of the park, the fairy light along the lawny spaces, the heavy perfume of the flowers, the pink of the camellias; and you quoted something: '*les camélias du balcon ressemblent à des désirs mourants*.' It was horrid of you: but you always had a knack of rubbing one up the wrong way. Then do you not remember how we danced in one room, while the servants set the other out with little tables? That supper was fascinating! I suppose it was these pleasant remembrances which made me wish for the shoes, but I could not summon up courage enough to buy them, and the horrid people were comparing me with the pastel; I suppose I did look a little mysterious with a double veil bound across my face. The shoes went with a lot of other things—and oh, to whom?

"So now that pretty little retreat in the *Rue de la Tour des Dames* is ended forever for you and me. We shall not see the faun in *terre cuite* again; I was thinking of going to see him the other day, but the street is so steep; my coachman advised me to spare the horse's hind legs. I believe it is the steepest street in Paris. And your luncheon parties, how I did enjoy them, and how Fay did enjoy them too; and what I risked, short-sighted as I am, picking my way from the tramcar down to that out-of-the-way little street! Men never appreciate the risks women run for them. But to leave my letters lying about—I cannot forgive that.

When I told Fay she said, 'What can you expect? I warned you against flirting with boys.' I never did before—never.

"Paris is now just as it was when you used to sit on the balcony and I read you Browning. You never liked his poetry, and I cannot understand why. I have found a new poem which I am sure would convert you; you should be here. There are lilacs in the room and the *Mont Valérien* is beautiful upon a great lemon sky, and the long avenue is merging into violet vapour.

"We have already begun to think of where we shall go to this year. Last year we went to P—, an enchanting place, quite rustic, but within easy distance of a casino. I had vowed not to dance, for I had been out every night during the season, but the temptation proved irresistible, and I gave way. There were two young men here, one the Count of B—, the other the Marquis of G—, one of the best families in France, a distant cousin of my husband. He has written a book which everyone says is one of the most amusing things that has appeared for years, *c'est surtout très Parisien*. He paid me great attentions, and made my husband wildly jealous. I used to go out and sit with him amid the rocks, and it was perhaps very lucky for me that he went away. We may return there this year; if so, I wish you would come and spend a month; there is an excellent hotel where you would be very comfortable. We have decided nothing as yet. The Duchesse de— is giving a costume ball; they say it is going to be a most wonderful affair. I don't know what money is not going to be spent upon the cotillion. I have just got home a fascinating toilette. I am going as a *Pierette*; you know, a short skirt and a little cap. The Marquise gave a ball some few days ago. I danced the cotillion with L—, who, as you know, dances divinely; *il m'a fait la cour*, but it is of course no use, you know that.

"The other night we went to see the *Maître-de-Forges*, a fascinating play, and I am reading the book; I don't know which I like the best. I think the play, but the book is very good too. Now that is what I call a novel; and I am a judge, for I have read all novels. But I must not talk literature, or you will say something stupid. I wish you would not make foolish remarks about men that *tout-Paris* considers the cleverest. It does not matter so much with me, I know you, but then people laugh at you behind your back, and that is not nice for me. The *marquise* was here the other day, and she said she almost wished you would not come on her 'days,' so extraordinary were the remarks you made. And by the way, the *marquise* has written a book. I have not seen it, but I hear that it is really too *décolleté*. She is *une femme d'esprit*, but the way she affiché's herself is too much for anyone. She never goes anywhere now without *le petit* D—. It is a great pity.

"And now, my dear friend, write me a nice letter, and tell me when you are coming back to Paris. I am sure you cannot amuse yourself in that hateful London; the nicest thing about you was that you were really *trés Parisien*. Come back and take a nice apartment on the Champs Elysées. You might come back for the Duchesse's ball. I will get an invitation for you, and will keep the cotillion for you. The idea of running away as you did, and never telling anyone where you were going to. I always said you were a little cracked. And letting all your things be sold! If you had only told me! I should like so much to have had that Turkish lamp. Yours—"

How like her that letter is,—egotistical, vain, foolish; no, not foolish—narrow, limited, but not foolish; worldly, oh, how worldly! and yet not repulsively so, for there always was in her a certain intensity of feeling that saved her from the commonplace, and gave her an inexpressible charm. Yes, she is a woman who can feel, and she has lived her life and felt it very acutely, very sincerely—sincerely? . . . like a moth caught in a gauze curtain! Well, would that preclude sincerity? Sincerity seems to convey an idea of depth, and she was not very deep, that is quite certain. I never could understand her;—a little brain that span rapidly and hummed a pretty humming tune. But no, there was something more in her than that. She often said things that I thought clever, things that I did not forget, things that I should like to put into books. But it was not brain power; it was only intensity of feeling—nervous feeling. I don't know. . . perhaps. . . She has lived her life. . . yes, within certain limits she has lived her life. None of us do more than that. True. I remember the first time I saw her. Sharp, little, and merry—a changeable little sprite. I thought she had ugly hands; so she has, and yet I forgot all about her hands before I had known her a month. It is now seven years ago. How time passes! I was very young then. What battles we have had, what quarrels! Still we had good times together. She never lost sight of me, but no intrusion; far too clever for that. I never got the better of her but once. . . once I did, *enfin*! She soon made up for lost ground. I wonder what the charm was. I did not think her pretty, I did not think her clever; that I know. . . I never knew if she cared for me, never. There were moments when. . . Curious, febrile, subtle little creature, oh, infinitely subtle, subtle in everything, in her sensations subtle; I suppose that was her charm, subtleness. I never knew if she cared for me, I never knew if she hated her husband,—one never knew her,—I never knew how she would receive me. The last time I saw her. . . that stupid American would take her downstairs, no getting rid of him, and I was hiding behind one of the pillars in the Rue de Rivoli, my hand on the cab door. However, she could not blame me that time—and all the stories she used to invent of my indiscretions; I believe she used to get them up for the sake of the excitement. She was awfully silly in some ways, once you got her into a certain line; that marriage, that title, and she used to think of it night and day. I shall never forget when she went into mourning for the Count de Chambord. And her tastes, oh, how bourgeois they were! That salon; the flagrantly modern clock, brass work, eight hundred francs on the Boulevard St Germain, the cabinets, brass work, the rich brown carpet, and the furniture set all round the room geometrically, the great gilt mirror, the ancestral portrait, the arms and crest everywhere, and the stuffy bourgeois sense of comfort; a little grotesque no doubt;—the mechanical admiration for all that is about her, for the general atmosphere; the *Figaro*, that is to say Albert Wolf, *l'homme le plus spirituel de Paris, c'est-à-dire, dans le monde*, the success of Georges Ohnet and the talent of Gustave Doré. But with all this vulgarity of taste certain appreciations, certain ebullitions of sentiment, within the radius of sentiment certain elevations and depravities,— depravities in the legitimate sense of the word, that is to say, a revolt against the commonplace. . .

Ha, ha, ha! how I have been dreaming! I wish I had not been awoke from my reverie, it was pleasant.

The letter just read indicates, if it does not clearly tell, the changes that have taken place in my life; and it is only necessary to say that one morning, a few months ago, when my servant brought me some summer honey and a glass of milk to my bedside, she handed me an unpleasant letter. My agent's handwriting, even when I knew the envelope contained a cheque, has never quite failed to produce a sensation of repugnance in me;—so hateful is any sort of account, that I avoid as much as possible even knowing how I stand at my banker's. Therefore the odour of honey and milk, so evocative of fresh flowers and fields, was spoilt that morning for me; and it was sometime before I slipped on that beautiful Japanese dressing-gown, which I shall never see again, and read the odious epistle.

That some wretched farmers and miners should refuse to starve, that I may not be deprived of my *demi-tasse* at *Tortoni's*, that I may not be forced to leave this beautiful retreat, my cat and my python—monstrous. And these wretched creatures will find moral support in England; they will find pity!

Pity, that most vile of all vile virtues, has never been known to me. The great pagan world I love knew it not. Now the world proposes to interrupt the terrible austere laws of nature which ordain that the weak shall be trampled upon, shall be ground into death and dust, that the strong shall be really strong,—that the strong shall be glorious, sublime. A little bourgeois comfort, a little bourgeois sense of right, cry the moderns.

Hither the world has been drifting since the coming of the pale socialist of Galilee; and this is why I hate Him, and deny His divinity. His divinity is falling, it is evanescent in sight of the goal He dreamed; again He is denied by His disciples. Poor fallen God! I, who hold nought else pitiful, pity Thee, Thy bleeding face and hands and feet, Thy hanging body; Thou at least art picturesque, and in a way beautiful in the midst of the sombre mediocrity, towards which Thou has drifted for two thousand years, a flag; and in which Thou shalt find Thy doom as I mine, I, who will not adore Thee and cannot curse Thee now. For verily Thy life and Thy fate has been greater, stranger and more Divine than any man's has been. The chosen people, the garden, the betrayal, the crucifixion, and the beautiful story, not of Mary, but of Magdalen. The God descending to the harlot! Even the great pagan world of marble and pomp and lust and cruelty, that my soul goes out to and hails as the grandest, has not so sublime a contrast to show us as this.

Come to me, ye who are weak. The Word went forth, the terrible disastrous Word, and before it fell the ancient gods, and the vices that they represent, and which I revere, are outcast now in the world of men; the Word went forth, and the world interpreted the Word, blindly, ignorantly, savagely, for two thousand years, but nevertheless nearing everyday the end—the end that Thou in Thy divine intelligence foresaw, that finds its voice today (enormous though the antithesis may be, I will say it) in the *Pall Mall Gazette*. What fate has been like Thine? Betrayed by Judas in the garden, denied by Peter before the cock crew, crucified between thieves, and mourned for by a harlot, and then sent bound and bare, nothing changed, nothing altered, in Thy ignominious plight, forthward in the world's van the glory and symbol of a man's new idea— Pity. Thy day is closing in, but the heavens are now wider aflame with Thy light than ever before—Thy light, which I, a pagan, standing on the last verge of the old world, declare to be darkness, the coming night of pity and justice which is imminent, which is the twentieth century. The bearers have relinquished Thy cross, they leave Thee in the hour of Thy universal triumph, Thy crown of thorns is falling, Thy face is buffeted with blows, and not even a reed is placed in Thy hand for sceptre; only I and mine are by Thee, we who shall perish with Thee, in the ruin Thou hast created.

Injustice we worship; all that lifts us out of the miseries of life is the sublime fruit of injustice. Every immortal deed was an act of fearful injustice; the world of grandeur, of triumph, of courage, of lofty aspiration, was built up on injustice. Man would not be man but for injustice. Hail, therefore, to the thrice glorious virtue injustice! What care I that some millions of wretched Israelites died under Pharaoh's lash or Egypt's sun? It was well that they died that I might have the pyramids to look on, or to fill a musing hour with wonderment. Is there one amongst us who would exchange them for the lives of the ignominious slaves that died? What care I that the virtue of some sixteen-year-old maiden was the price paid for Ingres' *La Source*? That the model died of drink and disease in the hospital, is nothing when compared with the essential that I should have *La Source*, that exquisite dream of innocence, to think of till my soul is sick with delight of the painter's holy vision. Nay more, the knowledge that a wrong was done— that millions of Israelites died in torments, that a girl, or a thousand girls, died in the hospital for that one virginal thing, is an added pleasure which I could not afford to spare. Oh, for the silence of marble courts, for the shadow of great pillars, for gold, for reticulated canopies of lilies; to see the great gladiators pass, to hear them cry the famous "Ave Caesar," to hold the thumb down, to see the blood flow, to fill the languid hours with the agonies of poisoned slaves! Oh, for excess, for crime! I would give many lives to save one sonnet by Baudelaire; for the hymn, "*A la très-chère, à la très-belle, qui remplit man cœur de clarté*" let the first-born in every house in Europe be slain; and in all sincerity I profess my readiness to decapitate all the Japanese in Japan and elsewhere, to save from destruction one drawing by Hokusai. Again I say that all we deem sublime in the world's history are acts of injustice; and it is certain that if mankind does not relinquish at once, and forever, its vain, mad, and fatal dream of justice, the world will lapse into barbarism. England was great and glorious, because England was unjust, and England's greatest son was the personification of injustice—Cromwell.

But the old world of heroes is over now. The skies above us are dark with sentimentalism, the sand beneath us is shoaling fast, we are running with streaming canvas upon ruin; all ideals have gone; nothing remains to us for worship but the Mass, the blind, inchoate, insatiate Mass; fog and fen land before us, we shall founder in putrefying mud, creatures of the ooze and rushes about us—we, the great ship that has floated up from the antique world. Oh, for the antique world, its plain passion, its plain joys in the sea, where the Triton blew a plaintive blast, and the forest where the whiteness of the nymph was seen escaping! We are weary of pity, we are weary of being good; we are weary of tears and effusion, and our refuge—the British Museum—is the wide sea shore and the wind of the ocean. There, there is real joy in the flesh; our statues are naked, but we are ashamed, and our nakedness is indecency: a fair, frank soul is mirrored in those fauns and nymphs; and how strangely enigmatic is the soul of the antique world, the bare, barbarous soul of beauty and of might!

XI

B ut neither Apollo nor Buddha could help or save me. One in his exquisite balance of body, a skylark-like song of eternal beauty, stood lightly advancing; the other sat in sombre contemplation, calm as a beautiful evening. I looked for sorrow in the eyes of the pastel— the beautiful pastel that seemed to fill with a real presence the rich autumnal leaves where the jays darted and screamed. The twisted columns of the bed rose, burdened with great weight of fringes and curtains, the python devoured a guinea-pig, the last I gave him; the great white cat came to me. I said all this must go, must henceforth be to me an abandoned dream, a something, not more real than a summer meditation. So be it, and, as was characteristic of me, I broke with Paris suddenly, without warning anyone. I knew in my heart of hearts that I should never return, but no word was spoken, and I continued a pleasant delusion with myself; I told my *concierge* that I would return in a month, and I left all to be sold, brutally sold by auction, as the letter I read in the last chapter charmingly and touchingly describes.

Not even to Marshall did I confide my foreboding that Paris would pass out of my life, that it would henceforth be with me a beautiful memory, but never more a practical delight. He and I were no longer living together; we had parted a second time, but this time without bitterness of any kind; he had learnt to feel that I wanted to live alone, and had moved away into the Latin quarter, whither I made occasional expeditions. I accompanied him once to the old haunts, but various terms of penal servitude had scattered our friends, and I could not interest myself in the new. Nor did Marshall himself interest me as he had once done. To my eager taste, he had grown just a little trite. My affection for him was as deep and sincere as ever; were I to meet him now I would grasp his hand and hail him with firm, loyal friendship; but I had made friends in the Nouvelle Athènes who interested me passionately, and my thoughts were absorbed by and set on new ideals, which Marshall had failed to find sympathy for, or even to understand. I had introduced him to Degas and Manet, but he had spoken of Jules Lefèbvre and Bouguereau, and generally shown himself incapable of any higher education; he could not enter where I had entered, and this was alienation. We could no longer even talk of the same people; when I spoke of a certain *marquise*, he answered with an indifferent "Do you really think so"? and proceeded to drag me away from my glitter of satin to the dinginess of print dresses. It was more than alienation, it was almost separation; but he was still my friend, he was the man, and he always will be, to whom my youth, with all its aspirations, was most closely united. So I turned to say goodbye to him and to my past life. Rap—rap—rap!

"Who's there?"

"I—George Moore."

"I've got a model."

"Never mind your model. Open the door. How are you? what are you painting?"

"This; what do you think of it?"

"It is prettily composed. I think it will come out all right. I am going to England; come to say goodbye."

"Going to England! What will you do in England?"

"I have to go about money matters, very tiresome. I had really begun to forget there was such a place."

"But you are not going to stay there?"

"Oh, no!"

"You will be just in time to see the Academy."

The conversation turned on art, and we æstheticised for an hour. At last Marshall said, "I am really sorry, old chap, but I must send you away; there's that model."

The girl sat waiting, her pale hair hanging down her back, a very picture of discontent.

"Send her away."

"I asked her to come out to dinner."

"D—n her. . . Well, never mind, I must spend this last evening with you; you shall both dine with me. *Je quitte Paris demain matin, peut-etre pour longtemps; je voudrais passer ma dernière soirèe avec mon ami; alors si vous voulez bien me permettre, mademoiselle, je vous invite tous les deux à diner; nous passerons la soirèe ensemble si cela vous est agrèable?*"

"*Je veux bien, monsieur.*"

Poor Marie! Marshall and I were absorbed in each other and art. It was always so. We dined in a *gargote*, and afterwards we went to a students' ball; and it seems like yesterday. I can see the moon sailing through a clear sky, and on the pavement's edge Marshall's beautiful, slim, manly figure, and Marie's exquisite gracefulness. She was Lefèbvre's Chloe; so everyone sees her now. Her end was a tragic one. She invited her friends to dinner, and with the few pence that remained she bought some boxes of matches, boiled them, and drank the water. No one knew why; some said it was love.

I went to London in an exuberant necktie, a tiny hat; I wore large trousers and a Capoul beard; looking, I believe, as unlike an Englishman as a drawing by Grévin. In the smoking-room of Morley's Hotel I met my agent, an immense nose, and a wisp of hair drawn over a bald skull. He explained, after some hesitation, that I owed him a few thousands, and that the accounts were in his portmanteau. I suggested taking them to a solicitor to have them examined. The solicitor advised me strongly to contest them. I did not take the advice, but raised some money instead, and so the matter ended so far as the immediate future was concerned. The years that are most impressionable, from twenty to thirty, when the senses and the mind are the widest awake, I, the most impressionable of human beings, had spent in France, not among English residents, but among that which is the quintessence of the nation, not an indifferent spectator, but an enthusiast, striving heart and soul to identify himself with his environment, to shake himself free from race and language and to recreate himself as it were in the womb of a new nationality, assuming its ideals, its morals, and its modes of thought, and I had succeeded strangely well, and when I returned home England was a new country to me; I had, as it were, forgotten everything. Every aspect of street and suburban garden was new to me; of the manner of life of Londoners I knew nothing. This sounds incredible, but it is so; I saw, but I could realise nothing. I went into a drawing-room, but everything seemed far away—a dream, a presentment, nothing more; I was in touch with nothing; of the thoughts and feelings of those I met I could understand nothing, nor could I sympathise with them: an Englishman was at that time as much out of my mental reach as an Esquimaux would be now. Women were nearer to me than men, and I will take this opportunity to note my observation, for I am not aware that anyone else has observed that the difference between the two races is found in the men, not in the women. French and English women are psychologically very similar; the standpoint from which they see life is the same, the same thoughts interest and amuse them; but the attitude of a Frenchman's mind is absolutely opposed to that of an Englishman; they stand on either side of a vast abyss, two animals different in colour, form, and temperament;—two ideas destined to remain irrevocably separate and distinct.

I have heard of writing and speaking two languages equally well: this was impossible to me, and I am convinced that if I had remained two more years in France I should never have been able to identify my thoughts with the language I am now writing in, and I should have written it as an alien. As it was I only just escaped this detestable fate. And it was in the last two years, when I began to write French verse and occasional *chroniques* in the papers, that the great damage was done. I remember very well indeed one day, while arranging an act of a play I was writing with a friend, finding suddenly to my surprise that I could think more easily and rapidly in French that in English; but with all this I did not learn French. I chattered, and I felt intensely at home in it; yes, I could write a sonnet or a ballade almost without a slip, but my prose required a good deal of alteration, for a greater command of language is required to write in prose than in verse. I found this in French and also in English. When I returned from Paris, my English terribly corrupt with French ideas and forms of thought, I could write acceptable English verse, but even ordinary newspaper prose was beyond my reach, and an attempt I made to write a novel drifted into a miserable failure.

Here is a poem that Cabaner admired; he liked it in the French prose translation which I made for him one night in the Nouvelle Athènes:—

We are alone! Listen, a little while,
And hear the reason why your weary smile
And lute-toned speaking is so very sweet,
And how my love of you is more complete
Than any love of any lover. They
Have only been attracted by the gray
Delicious softness of your eyes, your slim
And delicate form, or some such other whim,
The simple pretexts of all lovers;—I
For other reason. Listen whilst I try
To say. I joy to see the sunset slope
Beyond the weak hours' hopeless horoscope,
Leaving the heavens a melancholy calm
Of quiet colour chaunted like a psalm,
In mildly modulated phrases; thus
Your life shall fade like a voluptuous

Vision beyond the sight, and you shall die
Like some soft evening's sad serenity. . .
I would possess your dying hours; indeed
My love is worthy of the gift, I plead
For them. Although I never loved as yet,
Methinks that I might love you; I would get
From out the knowledge that the time was brief,
That tenderness, whose pity grows to grief,
And grief that sanctifies, a joy, a charm
Beyond all other loves, for now the arm
Of Death is stretched to you-ward, and he claims
You as his bride. Maybe my soul misnames
Its passion; love perhaps it is not, yet
To see you fading like a violet,
Or some sweet thought away, would be a strange
And costly pleasure, far beyond the range
Of formal man's emotion. Listen, I
Will choose a country spot where fields of rye
And wheat extend in rustling yellow plains,
Broken with wooded hills and leafy lanes,
To pass our honeymoon; a cottage where,
The porch and windows are festooned with fair
Green wreaths of eglantine, and look upon
A shady garden where we'll walk alone
In the autumn sunny evenings; each will see
Our walks grow shorter, till to the orange tree,
The garden's length, is far, and you will rest
From time to time, leaning upon my breast
Your languid lily face. Then later still
Unto the sofa by the window-sill
Your wasted body I shall carry, so
That you may drink the last left lingering glow
Of evening, when the air is filled with scent
Of blossoms; and my spirit shall be rent
The while with many griefs. Like some blue day
That grows more lovely as it fades away,
Gaining that calm serenity and height
Of colour wanted, as the solemn night
Steals forward you will sweetly fall asleep

Forever and forever; I shall weep
A day and night large tears upon your face,
Laying you then beneath a rose-red place
Where I may muse and dedicate and dream
Volumes of poesy of you; and deem
It happiness to know that you are far
From any base desires as that fair star
Set in the evening magnitude of heaven.
Death takes but little, yea, your death has given
Me that deep peace, and that secure possession
Which man may never find in earthly passion.

And here are two specimens of my French verse. I like to print them, for they tell me how I have held together, and they are not worse than my English verse, and is my English verse worse than the verse of our minor poets?

Nuit De Septembre

La nuit est pleine de silence,
Et dans une étrange lueur,
Et dans une douce indolence
La lune dort comme une fleur.

Parmi rochers, dans le sable
Sous les grands pins d'un calme amer
Surgit mon amour périssable,
Faim de tes yeux, soif de ta chair.

Je suis ton amant, et la blonde
Gorge tremble sous mon baiser,
Et le feu de l'amour inonde
Nos deux cœurs sans les apaiser.

Rien ne peut durer, mais ta bouche
Est telle qu'un fruit fait de sang;
Tout passe, mais ta main me touche
Et je me donne en frémissant,

Tes yeux verts me regardent: j'aime
Le clair de lune de tes yeux,
Et je ne vois dans le ciel même
Que ton corps rare et radieux.

Pour Un Tableau De Lord Leighton

De quoi rêvent-elles? de fleurs,
D'ombres, d'étoiles ou de pleurs?
De quoi rêvent ces douces femmes
De leurs amours ou de leurs âmes?

Parcilles aux lis abattus
Elles dorment les rêves tus
Dans la grande fenêtre ovale
Ou s'ouvre la nuit estivale.

But I realised before I was thirty that minor poetry is not sufficient occupation for a life-time—I realised that fact suddenly—I remember the very place at the corner of Wellington Street in the Strand; and these poems were the last efforts of my muse.

The Sweetness of the Past

As sailors watch from their prison
For the faint grey line of the coasts,
I look to the past re-arisen,
And joys come over in hosts
Like the white sea birds from their roosts.

I love not the indelicate present,
The future's unknown to our quest,
Today is the life of the peasant,
But the past is a haven of rest—
The things of the past are the best.

The rose of the past is better
Than the rose we ravish today,

'Tis holier, purer, and fitter
To place on the shrine where we pray
For the secret thoughts we obey.

In the past nothing dies, nothing changes,
In the past all is lovely and still;
No grief nor fate that estranges,
Nor hope that no life can fulfil,
But ethereal shelter from ill.

The coarser delights of the hour
Tempt, and debauch, and deprave,
And we joy in a flitting flower,
Knowing that nothing can save
Our flesh from the fate of the grave.

But sooner or later returning
In grief to the well-loved nest,
Our souls filled with infinite yearning,
We cry, there is rest, there is rest
In the past, its joys are the best.

Nostalgia

Fair were the dreamful days of old,
When in the summer's sleepy shade,
Beneath the beeches on the wold,
The shepherds lay and gently played
Music to maidens, who, afraid,
Drew all together rapturously,
Their white soft hands like white leaves laid,
In the old dear days of Arcady.

Men were not then as they are now
Haunted and terrified by creeds,
They sought not then, nor cared to know
The end that as a magnet leads,
Nor told with austere fingers beads,
Nor reasoned with their grief and glee,

But rioted in pleasant meads
In the old dear days of Arcady.

The future may be wrong or right,
The present is a hopeless wrong,
For life and love have lost delight,
And bitter even is our song;
And year by year grey doubt grows strong,
And death is all that seems to dree.
Wherefore with weary hearts we long
For the old dear days of Arcady.

Envoi.

Glories and triumphs ne'er shall cease,
But men may sound the heavens and sea,
One thing is lost for aye—the peace
Of the old dear days of Arcady.

And so it was that I came to settle down in a Strand lodging-house, determined to devote myself to literature, and to accept the hardships of a literary life. I had been playing long enough, and was now anxious for proof, peremptory proof, of my capacity or incapacity. A book! No. An immediate answer was required, and journalism alone could give that. So did I reason in the Strand lodging-house. And what led me to that house? Chance, or a friend's recommendation? I forget. It was uncomfortable, ugly, and not very clean; but curious, as all things are curious when examined closely. Let me tell you about my rooms. The sitting-room was a good deal longer than it was wide; it was panelled with deal, and the deal was painted a light brown; behind it there was a large bedroom: the floor was covered with a ragged carpet, and a big bed stood in the middle of the floor. But next to the sitting-room was a small bedroom which was let for ten shillings a week; and the partition wall was so thin that I could hear every movement the occupant made. This proximity was intolerable, and eventually I decided on adding ten shillings to my rent, and I became the possessor of the entire flat. In the room above me lived a pretty young woman, an actress at the Savoy Theatre. She had a piano, and she used to play and sing in the mornings, and in the afternoon, friends—girls from the theatre—used to come and see her; and Emma, the maid-of-all-work, used to take them up their tea; and, oh! the chattering and the laughter. Poor Miss L——; she had only two pounds a week to live on, but she was always in high spirits except when she could not pay the hire of her piano; and I am sure that she now looks back with pleasure and thinks of those days as very happy ones.

She was a tall girl, a thin figure, and she had large brown eyes; she liked young men, and she hoped that Mr. Gilbert would give her a line or two in his next opera. Often have I come out on the landing to meet her; we used to sit on those stairs talking, long after midnight, of what?—of our landlady, of the theatre, of the most suitable ways of enjoying ourselves in life. One night she told me she was married; it was a solemn moment. I asked in a sympathetic voice why she was not living with her husband. She told me, but the reason of the separation I have forgotten in the many similar reasons for separations and partings which have since been confided to me. The landlady resented our intimacy, and I believe Miss L—— was charged indirectly for her conversations with me in the bill. On the first floor there was a large sitting-room and bedroom, solitary rooms that were nearly always unlet. The landlady's parlour was on the ground floor, her bedroom was next to it, and further on was the entrance to the kitchen stairs, whence ascended Mrs. S——'s brood of children, and Emma, the awful servant, with tea things, many various smells, that of ham and eggs predominating.

Emma, I remember you—you are not to be forgotten—up at five o'clock every morning, scouring, washing, cooking, dressing those infamous children; seventeen hours at least out of the twenty-four at the beck and call of landlady, lodgers, and quarrelling children; seventeen hours at least out of the twenty-four drudging in that horrible kitchen, running up stairs with coals and breakfasts and cans of hot water; down on your knees before a grate, pulling out the cinders with those hands—can I call them hands? The lodgers sometimes threw you a kind word, but never one that recognised that you were akin to us, only the pity that might be extended to a dog. And I used to ask you all sorts of cruel questions, I was curious to know the depth of animalism you had sunk to, or rather out of which you had never been raised. And generally you answered innocently and naïvely enough. But sometimes my words were too crude, and they struck through the thick hide into the quick, into the human, and you winced a little; but this was rarely, for you were very nearly, oh, very nearly an animal, your temperament and intelligence were just those of a dog that has picked up a master, not a real master, but a makeshift master who may turn it out at any moment. Dickens would sentimentalise or laugh over you; I do neither. I merely recognise you as one of the facts of civilisation. You looked— well, to be candid,—you looked neither young nor old; hard work had obliterated the delicate markings of the years, and left you in round numbers something over thirty. Your hair was reddish brown, and your face wore that plain honest look that is so essentially English. The rest of you was a mass of stuffy clothes, and when you rushed up stairs I saw something that did not look like legs; a horrible rush that was of yours, a sort of cart-horselike bound. I have spoken angrily to you; I have heard others speak angrily to you, but never did that sweet face of yours, for it was a sweet face—that sweet, natural goodness that is so sublime—lose its expression of perfect and unfailing kindness. Words convey little sense of the real horrors of the reality. Life in your case meant this: to be born in a slum, and to leave it to work seventeen hours a day in a lodging-house; to be a Londoner, but to know only the slum in which you were born and the few shops in the Strand at which the landlady dealt. To know nothing of London meant in your case not to know that it was not England; England and London! you could not distinguish between them. Was England an island or a mountain? you had no notion. I remember when you heard that Miss L— was going to America, you asked me, and the question was sublime: "Is she going to travel all night?" You had heard people speak of travelling all night, and that was all you knew of travel or any place that was not the Strand. I asked you if you went to church, and you said, "No, it makes my eyes bad." I said, "But you don't read; you can't read." "No, but I have to look at the book." I asked you if you had heard of God— you hadn't, but when I pressed you on the point you suspected I was laughing at you, and you would not answer, and when I tried you again on the subject I could see that the landlady had been telling you what to say. But you had not understood, and your conscious ignorance, grown conscious within the last couple of days, was even more pitiful than your unconscious ignorance when you answered that you couldn't go to church because it made your eyes bad. It is a strange thing to know nothing; for instance, to live in London and to have no notion of the House of Commons, nor indeed of the Queen, except perhaps that she is a rich lady; the police—yes, you knew what a policeman was because you used to be sent to fetch one to make an organ-man or a Christy minstrel move on. To know of nothing but a dark kitchen, grates, eggs and bacon, dirty children; to work seventeen hours a day and to get cheated out of your wages; to answer, when asked, why you did not get your wages or leave if you weren't paid, that you "didn't know how Mrs. S— would get on without me."

This woman owed you forty pounds, I think, so I calculated it from what you told me; and yet you did not like to leave her because you did not know how she would get on without you. Sublime stupidity! At this point your intelligence stopped. I remember you once spoke of a half-holiday; I questioned you, and I found your idea of a half-holiday was to take the children for a walk and buy them some sweets. I told my brother of this and he said—Emma out for a half-holiday! why, you might as well give a mule a holiday. The phrase was brutal, but it was admirably descriptive of you. Yes, you are a mule, there is no sense in you; you are a beast of burden, a drudge too horrible for anything but work; and I suppose, all things considered, that the fat landlady with a dozen children did well to work you seventeen hours a day, and cheat you out of your miserable wages. You had no friends; you could not have a friend unless it were some forlorn cat or dog; but you once spoke to me of your brother, who worked in a potato store, and I was astonished, and I wondered if he were as awful as you. Poor Emma! I shall never forget your kind heart and your unfailing good humour; you were born beautifully good as a rose is born with perfect perfume; you were as unconscious of your goodness as the rose of its perfume. And you were taken by this fat landlady as 'Arry takes a rose and sticks it in his tobacco-reeking coat; and you will be thrown away, shut out of doors when health fails you, or when, overcome by base usage, you take to drink. There is no hope for you; even if you were treated better and paid your wages there would be no hope. Those forty pounds even, if they were given to you, would bring you no good fortune. They would bring the idle loafer, who scorns you now as something too low for even his kisses, hanging about your heels and whispering in your ears. And his whispering would drive you mad, for your kind heart longs for kind words; and then when he had spent your money and cast you off in despair, the gin shop and the river would do the rest. Providence is very wise after all, and your best destiny is your present one. We cannot add a pain, nor can we take away a pain; we may alter, but we cannot subtract nor even alleviate. But what truisms are these; who believes in philanthropy nowadays?

"Come in."

"Oh, it is you, Emma!"

"Are you going to dine at home today, sir?"

"What can I have?"

"Well, yer can 'ave a chop or a steak."

"Anything else?"

"Yes, yer can 'ave a steak, or a chop, or—"

"Oh, yes, I know; well then, I'll have a chop. And now tell me, Emma, how is your young man? I hear you have got one, you went out with him the other night."

"Who told yer that?"

"Ah, never mind; I hear everything."

"I know, from Miss L—"

"Well, tell me, how did you meet him, who introduced him?"

"I met 'im as I was a-coming from the public 'ouse with the beer for missus' dinner."

"And what did he say?"

"He asked me if I was engaged; I said no. And he come round down the lane that evening."

"And he took you out?"

"Yes."

"And where did you go?"

"We went for a walk on the Embankment."

"And when is he coming for you again?"

"He said he was coming last evening, but he didn't."

"Why didn't he?"

"I dunno; I suppose because I haven't time to go out with him. So it was Miss L— that told you; well, you do 'ave chats on the stairs. I suppose you likes talking to 'er."

"I like talking to everybody, Emma; I like talking to you."

"Yes, but not as you talks to 'er; I 'ears you jes do 'ave fine times. She said this morning that she had not seen you for this last two nights— that you had forgotten 'er, and I was to tell yer."

"Very well, I'll come out tonight and speak to her."

"And missus is so wild about it, and she daren't say nothing 'cause she thinks yer might go."

A young man in a house full of women must be almost supernaturally unpleasant if he does not occupy a great deal of their attention. Certain at least it is that I was the point of interest in that house; and I found there that the practice of virtue is not so disagreeable as many young men think it. The fat landlady hovered round my doors, and I obtained perfectly fresh eggs by merely keeping her at her distance; the pretty actress, with whom I used to sympathise with on the stairs at midnight, loved me better, and our intimacy was more strange and subtle, because it was pure, and it was not quite unpleasant to know that the awful servant dreamed of me as she might of a star, or something equally unattainable; but the landlady's daughter, a nasty girl of fifteen, annoyed me with her ogling, which was a little revolting, but the rest was, and I speak quite candidly, not wholly unpleasant. It was not aristocratic, it is true, but, I repeat, it was not unpleasant, nor do I believe that any young man, however refined, would have found it unpleasant.

But if I was offered a choice between a chop and steak in the evening, in the morning I had to decide between eggs and bacon and bacon and eggs. A knocking at the door, "Nine o'clock, sir; 'ot water, sir; what will you have for breakfast?" "What can I have?" "Anything you like, sir. You can have bacon and eggs, or—" "Anything else?"—Pause,—"Well, sir, you can have eggs and bacon, or—" "Well, I'll have eggs and bacon."

The streets seemed to me like rat holes, dark and wandering as chance directed, with just an occasional rift of sky, seen as if through an occasional crevice, so different from the boulevards widening out into bright space with fountains and clouds of green foliage. The modes of life were so essentially opposed. I am thinking now of intellectual rather than physical comforts. I could put up with even lodging-house food, but I found it difficult to forego the glitter and artistic enthusiasm of the *café*. The tavern, I had heard of the tavern.

Some seventy years ago the Club superseded the Tavern, and since then all literary intercourse has ceased in London. Literary clubs have been founded, and their leather arm-chairs have begotten Mr. Gosse; but the tavern gave the world Villon and Marlowe. Nor is this to be wondered at. What is wanted is enthusiasm and devil-may-careism; and the very aspect of a tavern is a snort of defiance at the hearth, the leather arm-chairs are so many salaams to it. I ask, Did anyone ever see a gay club room? Can anyone imagine such a thing? You can't have a club-room without mahogany tables, you can't have mahogany tables without magazines—*Longman's*, with a serial by Rider Haggard, the *Nineteenth Century*, with an article, "The Rehabilitation of the Pimp in Modern Society," by W. E. Gladstone—a dulness that's a purge to good spirits, an aperient to enthusiasm; in a word, a dulness that's worth a thousand a year. You can't have a club without a waiter in red plush and silver salver in his hand; then you can't bring a lady to a club, and you have to get into a corner to talk about them. Therefore I say a club is dull.

As the hearth and home grew all-powerful it became impossible for the husband to tell his wife that he was going to the tavern; everyone can go to the tavern, and no place in England where everyone can go is considered respectable. This is the genesis of the Club—out of the Housewife by Respectability. Nowadays everyone is respectable—jockeys, betting-men, actors, and even actresses. Mrs. Kendal takes her children to visit a duchess, and has naughty chorus girls to tea, and tells them of the joy of respectability. There is only one class left that is not respectable, and that will succumb before long; how the transformation will be effected I can't say, but I know an editor or two who would be glad of an article on the subject.

Respectability!—a suburban villa, a piano in the drawing-room, and going home to dinner. Such things are no doubt very excellent, but they do not promote intensity of feeling, fervour of mind; and as art is in itself an outcry against the animality of human existence, it would be well that the life of the artist should be a practical protest against the so-called decencies of life; and he can best protest by frequenting a tavern and cutting his club. In the past the artist has always been an outcast; it is only latterly he has become domesticated, and judging by results, it is clear that if Bohemianism is not a necessity it is at least an adjuvant. For if long locks and general dissoluteness were not an aid and a way to pure thought, why have they been so long his characteristics? If lovers were not necessary for the development of poet, novelist, and actress, why have they always had lovers—Sappho, George Eliot, George Sand, Rachel, Sara? Mrs. Kendal nurses children all day and strives to play Rosalind at night. What infatuation, what ridiculous endeavour! To realise the beautiful woodland passion and the idea of the transformation, a woman must have sinned, for only through sin may we learn the charm of innocence. To play Rosalind a woman must have had more than one lover, and if she has been made to wait in the rain and has been beaten she will have done a great deal to qualify herself for the part. The ecstatic Sara makes no pretence to virtue, she introduces her son to an English duchess, and throws over a nation for the love of Richepin, she can, therefore, say as none other—

"Ce n'est plus qu'une ardeur dans mes veines cachée,
C'est Venus tout entière à sa proie attachée."

Swinburne, when he dodged about London, a lively young dog, wrote "Poems and Ballads," and "Chastelard," since he has gone to live at Putney, he has contributed to the *Nineteenth Century*, and published an interesting little volume entitled, "A Century of Rondels," in which he continues his plaint about his mother the sea.

Respectability is sweeping the picturesque out of life; national costumes are disappearing. The kilt is going or gone in the highlands, and the smock in the southlands, even the Japanese are becoming christian and respectable; in another quarter of a century silk hats and pianos will be found in every house in Yeddo. Too true that universal uniformity is the future of the world; and when Mr. Morris speaks of the democratic art to be when the world is socialistic, I ask, whence will the unfortunates draw their inspiration? Today our plight is pitiable enough—the duke, the jockey-boy, and the artist are exactly alike; they are dressed by the same tailor, they dine at the same clubs, they swear the same oaths, they speak equally bad English, they love the same women. Such a state of things is dreary enough, but what unimaginable dreariness there will be when there are neither rich nor poor, when all have been educated, when self-education has ceased. A terrible world to dream of, worse, far worse, in darkness and hopelessness than Dante's lowest circle of hell. The spectre of famine, of the plague, of war, etc., are mild and gracious symbols compared with that menacing figure, Universal Education, with which we are threatened, which has already eunuched the genius of the last five-and-twenty years of the nineteenth century, and produced a limitless abortion in that of future time. Education, I tremble before thy dreaded name. The cruelties of Nero, of Caligula, what were they?—a few crunched limbs in the amphitheatre; but thine, O Education, are the yearning of souls sick of life, of maddening discontent, of all the fearsome and fathomless sufferings of the mind. When Goethe said "More light," he said the wickedest and most infamous words that human lips ever spoke. In old days, when a people became too highly civilised the barbarians came down from the north and regenerated that nation with darkness; but now there are no more barbarians, and sooner or later I am convinced that we shall have to end the evil by summary edicts—the obstruction no doubt will be severe, the equivalents of Gladstone and Morley will stop at nothing to defeat the Bill; but it will nevertheless be carried by patriotic Conservative and Unionist majorities, and it will be written in the Statute Book that not more than one child in a hundred shall be taught to read, and no more than one in ten thousand shall learn the piano.

Such will be the end of Respectability, but the end is still far distant. We are now in a period of decadence growing steadily more and more acute. The old gods are falling about us, there is little left to raise our hearts and minds to, and amid the wreck and ruin of things only a snobbery is left to us, thank heaven, deeply graven in the English heart; the snob is now the ark that floats triumphant over the democratic wave; the faith of the old world reposes in his breast, and he shall proclaim it when the waters have subsided.

In the meanwhile Respectability, having destroyed the Tavern, and created the Club, continues to exercise a meretricious and enervating influence on literature. All audacity of thought and expression has been stamped out, and the conventionalities are rigorously respected. It has been said a thousand times that an art is only a reflection of a certain age; quite so, only certain ages are more interesting than others, and consequently produce better art, just as certain seasons produce better crops. We heard in the Nouvelle Athènes how the Democratic movement, in other words, Respectability, in other words, Education, has extinguished the handicrafts; it was admitted that in the more individual arts—painting and poetry—men would be always found to sacrifice their lives for a picture or a poem: but no man is, after all, so immeasurably superior to the age he lives in as to be able to resist it wholly; he must draw sustenance from some quarter, and the contemplation of the past will not suffice. Then the pressure on him from without is as water upon the diver; and sooner or later he grows fatigued and comes to the surface to breathe; he is as a flying-fish pursued by sharks below and cruel birds above; and he neither dives as deep nor flies as high as his freer and stronger ancestry. A daring spirit in the nineteenth century would have been but a timid nursery soul indeed in the sixteenth. We want tumult and war to give us forgetfulness, sublime moments of peace to enjoy a kiss in; but we are expected to be home to dinner at seven, and to say and do nothing that might shock the neighbours. Respectability has wound itself about society, a sort of octopus, and nowhere are you quite free from one of its horrible suckers. The power of the villa residence is supreme: art, science, politics, religion, it has transformed to suit its requirements. The villa goes to the Academy, the villa goes to the theatre, and therefore the art of today is mildly realistic; not the great realism of idea, but the puny reality of materialism; not the deep poetry of a Peter de Hogue, but the meanness of a Frith— not the winged realism of Balzac, but the degrading naturalism of a coloured photograph.

To my mind there is no sadder spectacle of artistic debauchery than a London theatre; the overfed inhabitants of the villa in the stalls hoping for gross excitement to assist them through their hesitating digestions; an ignorant mob in the pit and gallery forgetting the miseries of life in imbecile stories reeking of the sentimentality of the back stairs. Were other ages as coarse and common as ours? It is difficult to imagine Elizabethan audiences as not more intelligent than those that applaud Mr. Pettit's plays. Impossible that an audience that could sit out Edward II could find any pleasure in such sinks of literary infamies as *In the Ranks* and *Harbour Lights*. Artistic atrophy is benumbing us, we are losing our finer feeling for beauty, the rose is going back to the briar. I will not speak of the fine old crusted stories, ever the same, on which every drama is based, nor yet of the musty characters with which they are peopled—the miser in the old castle counting his gold by night, the dishevelled woman whom he keeps for ambiguous reasons confined in a cellar. Let all this be waived. We must not quarrel with the ingredients. The miser and the old castle are as true, and not one jot more true, than the million events which go to make up the phenomena of human existence. Not at these things considered separately do I take umbrage, but at the miserable use that is made of them, the vulgarity of the complications evolved from them, and the poverty of beauty in the dialogue.

Not the thing itself, but the idea of the thing evokes the idea. Schopenhauer was right; we do not want the thing, but the idea of the thing. The thing itself is worthless; and the moral writers who embellish it with pious ornamentation are just as reprehensible as Zola, who embellishes it with erotic arabesques. You want the idea drawn out of obscuring matter, and this can best be done by the symbol. The symbol, or the thing itself, that is the great artistic question. In earlier ages it was the symbol; a name, a plume, sufficed to evoke the idea; now we evoke nothing, for we give everything, the imagination of the spectator is no longer called into play. In Shakespeare's days to create wealth in a theatre it was only necessary to write upon a board, "A magnificent apartment in a palace." This was no doubt primitive and not a little barbarous, but it was better by far than by dint of anxious archæology to construct the Doge's palace upon the stage. By one rich pillar, by some projecting balustrade taken in conjunction with a moored gondola, we should strive to evoke the soul of the city of Veronese: by the magical and unequalled selection of a subtle and unexpected feature of a thought or aspect of a landscape, and not by the up-piling of extraneous detail, are all great poetic effects achieved.

> *"By the tideless dolorous inland sea,*
> *In a land of sand, of ruin, and gold."*

And, better example still,

> *"Dieu que le son du cor est triste au fond des bois,"*

that impeccable, that only line of real poetry Alfred de Vigny ever wrote. Being a great poet Shakespeare consciously or unconsciously observed more faithfully than any other poet these principles of art; and, as is characteristic of the present day, nowhere do we find these principles so grossly violated as in the representation of his plays. I had painful proof of this some few nights after my arrival in London. I had never seen Shakespeare acted, and I went to the Lyceum and there I saw that exquisite love-song—for *Romeo and Juliet* is no more than a love song in dialogue—tricked out in silks and carpets and illuminated building, a vulgar bawd suited to the gross passion of an ignorant public. I hated all that with the hatred of a passionate heart, and I longed for a simple stage, a few simple indications, and the simple recitation of that story of the sacrifice of the two white souls for the reconciliation of two great families. My hatred did not reach to the age of the man who played the boy-lover, but to the offensiveness with which he thrust his individuality upon me, longing to realise the poet's divine imagination: and the woman, too, I wished with my whole soul away, subtle and strange though she was, and I yearned for her part to be played by a youth as in old time: a youth cunningly disguised, would be a symbol; and my mind would be free to imagine the divine Juliet of the poet, whereas I could but dream of the bright eyes and delicate mien and motion of the woman who had thrust herself between me and it.

But not with symbol and subtle suggestion has the villa to do, but with such stolid, intellectual fare as corresponds to its material wants. The villa has not time to think, the villa is the working bee. The tavern is the drone. It has no boys to put to school, no neighbours to study, and is therefore a little more refined, or, should I say? depraved, in its taste. The villa in one form or other has always existed, and always will exist so long as our present social system holds together. It is the basis of life, and more important than the tavern. Agreed: but that does not say that the tavern was not an excellent corrective influence to the villa, and that its disappearance has not had a vulgarising effect on artistic work of all kinds, and the club has been proved impotent to replace it, the club being no more than the correlative of the villa. Let the reader trace villa through each modern feature. I will pass on at once to the circulating library, at once the symbol and glory of villaism.

The subject is not unfamiliar to me; I come to it like the son to his father, like the bird to its nest. (Singularly inappropriate comparison, but I am in such excellent humour today; humour is everything. It is said that the tiger will sometimes play with the lamb! Let us play.) We have the villa well in our mind. The father who goes to the city in the morning, the grown-up girls waiting to be married, the big drawing-room where they play waltz music, and talk of dancing parties. But waltzes will not entirely suffice, nor even tennis; the girls must read. Mother cannot keep a censor (it is as much as she can do to keep a cook, housemaid and page-boy), besides the expense would be enormous, even if nothing but shilling and two-shilling novels were purchased. Out of such circumstances the circulating library was hatched.

The villa made known its want, and art fell on its knees. Pressure was put on the publishers, and books were published at 31s. 6d.; the dirty outside public was got rid of, and the villa paid its yearly subscription, and had nice large handsome books that none but the *élite* could obtain, and with them a sense of being put on a footing of equality with my Lady This and Lady That, and certainty that nothing would come into the hands of dear Kate and Mary and Maggie that they might not read, and all for two guineas a year. English fiction became pure, and the garlic and assafœtida with which Byron, Fielding and Ben Jonson so liberally seasoned their works, and in spite of which, as critics say, they were geniuses, have disappeared from our literature. English fiction became pure, dirty stories were to be heard no more, were no longer procurable. But at this point human nature intervened; poor human nature! when you pinch it in one place it bulges out in another, after the fashion of a lady's figure. Human nature has from the earliest time shown a liking for dirty stories; dirty stories have formed a substantial part of every literature (I employ the words "dirty stories" in the circulating library sense); therefore a taste for dirty stories may be said to be inherent in the human animal. Call it a disease if you will—an incurable disease—which, if it is driven inwards, will break out in an unexpected quarter in a new form and with redoubled virulence. This is exactly what has happened. Actuated by the most laudable motives, Mudie cut off our rations of dirty stories, and for forty years we were apparently the most moral people on the face of the earth. It was confidently asserted that an English woman of sixty would not read what would bring the blush of shame to the cheeks of a maiden of any other nation. But humiliation and sorrow were awaiting Mudie. True it is that we still continued to subscribe to his library, true it is that we still continued to go to church, true it is that we turned our faces away when *Mdlle. de Maupin* or the *Assommoir* was spoken of; to all appearance we were as good and chaste as even Mudie might wish us; and no doubt he looked back upon his forty years of effort with pride; no doubt he beat his manly breast and said, "I have scorched the evil one out of the villa; the head of the serpent is crushed for evermore"; but lo, suddenly, with all the horror of an earthquake, the slumbrous law courts awoke, and the burning cinders of fornication and the blinding and suffocating smoke of adultery were poured upon and hung over the land. Through the mighty columns of our newspapers the terrible lava rolled unceasing, and in the black stream the villa, with all its beautiful illusions, tumbled and disappeared.

An awful and terrifying proof of the futility of human effort, that there is neither bad work nor good work to do, nothing but to await the coming of the Nirvana.

I have written much against the circulating library, and I have read a feeble defence or two; but I have not seen the argument that might be legitimately put forward in its favour. It seems to me this: the circulating library is conservatism, art is always conservative; the circulating library lifts the writer out of the precariousness and noise of the wild street of popular fancy into a quiet place where passion is more restrained and there is more reflection. The young and unknown writer is placed at once in a place of comparative security, and he is not forced to employ vile and degrading methods of attracting attention; the known writer, having a certain market for his work, is enabled to think more of it and less of the immediate acclamation of the crowd; but all these possible advantages are destroyed and rendered *nil* by the veracious censorship exercised by the librarian.

THERE IS ONE THING IN England that is free, that is spontaneous, that reminds me of the blitheness and nationalness of the Continent;—but there is nothing French about it, it is wholly and essentially English, and in its communal enjoyment and its spontaneity it is a survival of Elizabethan England—I mean the music-hall; the French music-hall seems to me silly, effete, sophisticated, and lacking, not in the popularity, but in the vulgarity of an English hall—I will not say the Pavilion, which is too cosmopolitan, dreary French comics are heard there—for preference let us say the Royal. I shall not easily forget my first evening there, when I saw for the time a living house—the dissolute paragraphists, the elegant mashers (mark the imaginativeness of the slang), the stolid, good-humoured costers, the cheerful lights o' love, the extraordinary comics. What delightful unison of enjoyment, what unanimity of soul, what communality of wit; all knew each other, all enjoyed each other's presence; in a word, there was life. Then there were no cascades of real water, nor London docks, nor offensively rich furniture, with hotel lifts down which someone will certainly be thrown, but one scene representing a street; a man comes on—not, mind you, in a real smock-frock, but in something that suggests one—and sings of how he came up to London, and was "cleaned out" by thieves. Simple, you will say; yes, but better than a *fricassée* of *Faust*, garnished with hags, imps, and blue flame; better, far better than a drawing-room set at the St James's, with an exhibition of passion by Mrs. and Mr. Kendal; better, a million times better than the cheap popularity of Wilson Barrett—an elderly man posturing in a low-necked dress to some poor trull in the gallery; nor is there in the hall any affectation of language, nor that worn-out rhetoric which reminds you of a broken-winded barrel-organ playing *a che la morte*, bad enough in prose, but when set up in blank verse awful and shocking in its more than natural deformity—but bright quips and cranks fresh from the back-yard of the slum where the linen is drying, or the "pub" where the unfortunate wife has just received a black eye that will last her a week. That inimitable artist, Bessie Bellwood, whose native wit is so curiously accentuated that it is sublimated, that it is no longer repellent vulgarity but art, choice and rare—see, here she comes with "What cheer, Rea! Rea's on the job." The sketch is slight, but is welcome and refreshing after the eternal drawing-room and Mrs. Kendal's cumbrous domesticity; it is curious, quaint, perverted, and are not these the *aions* and the attributes of art? Now see that perfect comedian, Arthur Roberts, superior to Irving because he is working with living material; how trim and saucy he is! and how he evokes the soul, the brandy-and-soda soul, of the young men, delightful and elegant in black and white, who are so vociferously cheering him, "Will you stand me a cab-fare, ducky, I am feeling so awfully queer?" The soul, the spirit, the entity of Piccadilly Circus is in the words, and the scene the comedian's eyes—each look is full of suggestion; it is irritating, it is magnetic, it is symbolic, it is art.

Not art, but a sign, a presentiment of an art, that may grow from the present seeds, that may rise into some stately and unpremeditated efflorescence, as the rhapsodist rose to Sophocles, as the miracle play rose through Peele and Nash to Marlowe, hence to the wondrous summer of Shakespeare, to die later on in the mist and yellow and brown of the autumn of Crowes and Davenants. I have seen music-hall sketches, comic interludes that in their unexpectedness and naïve naturalness remind me of the comic passages in Marlowe's *Faustus*, I waited (I admit in vain) for some beautiful phantom to appear, and to hear an enthusiastic worshipper cry out in his agony:—

> *"Was this the face that launched a thousand ships*
> *And burnt the topless towers of Ilium?*
> *Sweet Helen, make me immortal with a kiss.*
> *Her lips suck forth my soul; see where it flies!*
> *Come, Helen, come; give me my soul again.*
> *Here will I dwell, for heaven is in these lips,*
> *And all is dross that is not Helena."*

And then the astonishing change of key:—

> *"I will be Paris, and for love of thee,*
> *Instead of Troy shall Wurtemberg be sacked," etc.*

The hall is at least a protest against the wearisome stories concerning wills, misers in old castles, lost heirs, and the woeful solutions of such things—she who has been kept in the castle cellar for twenty years restored to the delights of hair-pins and a mauve dress, the *ingenue* to the protecting arm, etc. The music-hall is a protest against Mrs. Kendal's marital tendernesses and the abortive platitudes of Messrs. Pettit and Sims; the music-hall is a protest against Sardou and the immense drawing-room sets, rich hangings, velvet sofas, etc., so different from the movement of the English comedy with its constant change of scene. The music-hall is a protest against the villa, the circulating library, the club, and for this the "'all" is inexpressibly dear to me.

But in the interests of those illiterate institutions called theatres it is not permissible for several characters to narrate events in which there is a sequel, by means of dialogue, in a music-hall. If this vexatious restriction were removed it is possible, if it is not certain, that while some halls remained faithful to comic songs and jugglers others would gradually learn to cater for more intellectual and subtle audiences, and that out of obscurity and disorder new dramatic forms, coloured and permeated by the thought and feeling of today, might be definitely evolved. It is our only chance of again possessing a dramatic literature.

XII

It is said that young men of genius come to London with great poems and dramas in their pockets and find every door closed against them. Chatterton's death perpetuated this legend. But when I, George Moore, came to London in search of literary adventure, I found a ready welcome. Possibly I should not have been accorded any welcome had I been anything but an ordinary person. Let this be waived. I was as covered with "fads" as a distinguished foreigner with stars. Naturalism I wore round my neck, Romanticism was pinned over the heart, Symbolism I carried like a toy revolver in my waistcoat pocket, to be used on an emergency. I do not judge whether I was charlatan or genius, I merely state that I found all—actors, managers, editors, publishers, docile and ready to listen to me. The world may be wicked, cruel, and stupid, but it is patient; on this point I will not be gainsaid, it is patient; I know what I am talking about; I maintain that the world is patient. If it were not, what would have happened? I should have been murdered by the editors of (I will suppress names), torn in pieces by the sub-editors, and devoured by the office boys. There was no wild theory which I did not assail them with, there was no strange plan for the instant extermination of the Philistine, which I did not press upon them, and (here I must whisper), with a fair amount of success, not complete success I am glad to say—that would have meant for the editors a change from their arm-chairs to the benches of the Union and the plank beds of Holloway. The actress, when she returned home from the theatre, suggested I had an enemy, a vindictive enemy, who dogged my steps; but her stage experience led her astray. I had no enemy except myself; or to put it scientifically, no enemy except the logical consequences of my past life and education, and these caused me a great and real inconvenience. French wit was in my brain, French sentiment was in my heart; of the English soul I knew nothing, and I could not remember old sympathies, it was like seeking forgotten words, and if I were writing a short story, I had to return in thought to Montmartre or the Champs Elysées for my characters. That I should have forgotten so much in ten years seems incredible, and it will be deemed impossible by many, but that is because few are aware of how little they know of the details of life, even of their own, and are incapable of appreciating the influence of their past upon their present. The visible world is visible only to a few, the moral world is a closed book to nearly all. I was full of France, and France had to be got rid of, or pushed out of sight before I could understand England; I was like a snake striving to slough its skin.

Handicapped as I was with dangerous ideas, and an impossible style, defeat was inevitable. My English was rotten with French idiom; it was like an ill-built wall overpowered by huge masses of ivy; the weak foundations had given way beneath the weight of the parasite; and the ideas I sought to give expression to were green, sour, and immature as apples in August.

Therefore before long the leading journal that had printed two poems and some seven or eight critical articles, ceased to send me books for review, and I fell back upon obscure society papers. Fortunately it was not incumbent on me to live by my pen; so I talked, and watched, and waited till I grew akin to those around me, and my thoughts blended with, and took root in my environment. I wrote a play or two, I translated a French opera, which had a run of six nights, I dramatized a novel, I wrote short stories, and I read a good deal of contemporary fiction.

The first book that came under my hand was "A Portrait of a Lady," by Henry James. Each scene is developed with complete foresight and certainty of touch. What Mr. James wants to do he does. I will admit that an artist may be great and limited; by one word he may light up an abyss of soul; but there must be this one magical and unique word. Shakespeare gives us the word, Balzac, sometimes, after pages of vain striving, gives us the word, Tourgueneff gives it with miraculous certainty; but Henry James, no; a hundred times he flutters about it; his whole book is one long flutter near to the one magical and unique word, but the word is not spoken; and for want of the word his characters are never resolved out of the haze of nebulae. You are on a bowing acquaintance with them; they pass you in the street, they stop and speak to you, you know how they are dressed, you watch the colour of their eyes. When I think of "A Portrait of a Lady," with its marvellous crowd of well-dressed people, it comes back to me precisely as an accurate memory of a fashionable soirée—the staircase with its ascending figures, the hostess smiling, the host at a little distance with his back turned; someone calls him. He turns; I can see his white kid gloves, the air is sugar sweet with the odour of the gardenias, there is brilliant light here, there is shadow in the further rooms, the women's feet pass to and fro beneath the stiff skirts, I call for my hat and coat,

I light a cigar, I stroll up Piccadilly. . . a very pleasant evening, I have seen a good many people I knew, I have observed an attitude, and an earnestness of manner that proved that a heart was beating.

Mr James might say, "If I have done this, I have done a great deal," and I would answer, "No doubt you are a man of great talent, great cultivation and not at all of the common herd; I place you in the very front rank, not only of novelists but of men of letters."

I have read nothing of Henry James's that did suggest the manner of a scholar; but why should a scholar limit himself to empty and endless sentimentalities? I will not taunt him with any of the old taunts—why does he not write complicated stories? Why does he not complete his stories? Let all this be waived. I will ask him only why he always avoids decisive action? Why does a woman never say "I will"? Why does a woman never leave the house with her lover? Why does a man never kill a man? Why does a man never kill himself? Why is nothing ever accomplished? In real life murder, adultery, and suicide are of common occurrence; but Mr. James's people live in a calm, sad, and very polite twilight of volition. Suicide or adultery has happened before the story begins, suicide or adultery happens some years hence, when the characters have left the stage, but in front of the reader nothing happens. The suppression or maintenance of story in a novel is a matter of personal taste; some prefer character-drawing to adventures, some adventures to character-drawing; that you cannot have both at once I take to be a self-evident proposition; so when Mr. Lang says, "I like adventures," I say, "Oh, do you?" as I might to a man who says "I like sherry," and no doubt when I say I like character-drawing, Mr. Lang says, "Oh, do you?" as he might to a man who says, "I like port." But Mr. James and I are agreed on essentials, we prefer character-drawing to adventures. One, two, or even three determining actions are not antagonistic to character-drawing, the practice of Balzac, and Flaubert, and Thackeray prove that. Is Mr. James of the same mind as the poet Verlaine—

> *"La nuance, pas la couleur,*
> *Seulement la nuance,*
>
> *. . . .*
> *Tout le reste est littérature."*

In connection with Henry James I had often heard the name of W.D. Howells. I bought some three or four of his novels. I found them pretty, very pretty, but nothing more,—a sort of Ashby Sterry done into very neat prose. He is vulgar, as Henry James is refined; he is more domestic; girls with white dresses and virginal looks, languid mammas, mild witticisms, here, there, and everywhere; a couple of young men, one a little cynical, the other a little over-shadowed by his love, a strong, bearded man of fifty in the background; in a word, a Tom Robertson comedy faintly spiced with American. Henry James went to France and read Tourgueneff. W.D. Howells stayed at home and read Henry James. Henry James's mind is of a higher cast and temper; I have no doubt at one time of his life Henry James said, I will write the moral history of America, as Tourgueneff wrote the moral history of Russia—he borrowed at first hand, understanding what he was borrowing. W.D. Howells borrowed at second hand, and without understanding what he was borrowing. Altogether Mr. James's instincts are more scholarly. Although his reserve irritates me, and I often regret his concessions to the prudery of the age,—no, not of the age but of librarians,—I cannot but feel that his concessions, for I suppose I must call them concessions, are to a certain extent self-imposed, regretfully, perhaps. . . somewhat in this fashion—"True, that I live in an age not very favourable to artistic production, but the art of an age is the spirit of that age; if I violate the prejudices of the age I shall miss its spirit, and an art that is not redolent of the spirit of its age is an artificial flower, perfumeless, or perfumed with the scent of flowers that bloomed three hundred years ago." Plausible, ingenious, quite in the spirit of Mr. James's mind; I can almost hear him reason so; nor does the argument displease me, for it is conceived in a scholarly spirit. Now my conception of W.D. Howells is quite different—I see him the happy father of a numerous family; the sun is shining, the girls and boys are playing on the lawn, they come trooping in to high tea, and there is dancing in the evening.

My fat landlady lent me a novel by George Meredith,—"Tragic Comedians"; I was glad to receive it, for my admiration of his poetry, with which I was slightly acquainted, was very genuine indeed. "Love in a Valley" is a beautiful poem, and the "Nuptials of Attila," I read it in the *New Quarterly Review* years ago, is very present in my mind, and it is a pleasure to recall its chanting rhythm, and lordly and sombre refrain—"Make the bed for Attila." I expected, therefore, one of my old passionate delights from his novels. I was disappointed, painfully disappointed. But before I say more concerning Mr. Meredith, I will admit at once frankly and fearlessly, that I am not a competent critic, because emotionally I do not understand him, and all except an emotional understanding is worthless in art. I do not make this admission because I am intimidated by the weight and height of the critical authority with which I am overshadowed, but from a certain sense, of which I am as distinctly conscious, viz., that the author is, how shall I put it? the French would say "quelqu'un," that expresses what I would say in English. I remember, too, that although a man may be able to understand anything, there must be some modes of thoughts and attitudes of mind which we are so naturally antagonistic to, so entirely out of sympathy with, that we are in no true sense critics of them. Such are the thoughts that come to me when I read Mr. George Meredith. I try to console myself with such reflections, and then I break out and cry passionately:—jerks, wire splintered wood. In Balzac, which I know by heart, in Shakespeare, which I have just begun to love, I find words deeply impregnated with the savour of life; but in George Meredith there is nothing but crackjaw sentences, empty and unpleasant in the mouth as sterile nuts. I could select hundreds of phrases which Mr. Meredith would probably call epigrams, and I would defy anyone to say they were wise, graceful or witty. I do not know any book more tedious than "Tragic Comedians," more pretentious, more blatant; it struts and screams, stupid in all its gaud and absurdity as a cockatoo. More than fifty pages I could not read. How, I asked myself, could the man who wrote the "Nuptials of Attila" write this? but my soul returned no answer, and I listened as one in a hollow mountain side. My opinion of George Meredith never ceases to puzzle me. He is of the north, I am of the south. Carlyle, Mr. Robert Browning, and George Meredith are the three essentially northern writers; in them there is nothing of Latin sensuality and subtlety.

I took up "Rhoda Fleming." I found some exquisite bits of description in it, but I heartily wished them in verse, they were motives for poems; and there was some wit. I remember a passage very racy indeed, of middle-class England. Antony, I think, is the man's name, describes how he is interrupted at his tea; a paragraph of seven or ten lines with "I am having my tea, I am at my tea," running through it for refrain. Then a description of a lodging-house dinner: "a block of bread on a lonely place, and potatoes that looked as if they had committed suicide in their own steam." A little ponderous and stilted, but undoubtedly witty. I read on until I came to a young man who fell from his horse, or had been thrown from his horse, I never knew which, nor did I feel enough interest in the matter to make research; the young man was put to bed by his mother, and once in bed he began to talk! . . . four, five, six, ten pages of talk, and such talk! I can offer no opinion why Mr. George Meredith committed them to paper; it is not narrative, it is not witty, nor is it sentimental, nor is it profound. I read it once; my mind, astonished at receiving no sensation, cried out like a child at a milkless breast. I read the pages again. . . did I understand? Yes, I understood every sentence, but they conveyed no idea, they awoke no emotion in me; it was like sand, arid and uncomfortable. The story is surprisingly commonplace—the people in it are as lacking in subtlety as those of a Drury Lane melodrama.

"Diana of the Crossways" I liked better, and had I had absolutely nothing to do I might have read it to the end. I remember a scene with a rustic—a rustic who could eat hog a solid hour—that amused me. I remember the sloppy road in the Weald, and the vague outlines of the South Downs seen in starlight and mist. But to come to the great question, the test by which Time will judge us all—the creation of a human being, of a live thing that we have met with in life before, and meet for the first time in print, and who abides with us ever after. Into what shadow has not Diana floated? Where are the magical glimpses of the soul? Do you remember in "Pères et Enfants," when Tourgueneff is unveiling the woman's, shall I say, affection, for Bazaroff, or the interest she feels in him? and exposing at the same time the reasons why she will never marry him. . . I wish I had the book by me, I have not seen it for ten years.

After striving through many pages to put Lucien, whom you would have loved, whom I would have loved, that divine representation of all that is young and desirable in man, before the reader, Balzac puts these words in his mouth in reply to an impatient question by Vautrin, who asks him what he wants, what he is sighing for, "*D'être célèbre et d'être aimè*,"—these are soul-waking words, these are Shakespearean words.

Where in "Diana of the Crossways" do we find soul-evoking words like these? With tiresome repetition we are told that she is beautiful, divine; but I see her not at all, I don't know if she is dark, tall, or fair; with tiresome reiteration we are told that she is brilliant, that her conversation is like a display of fireworks, that the company is dazzled and overcome; but when she speaks the utterances are grotesque, and I say that if anyone spoke to me in real life as she does in the novel, I should not doubt for an instant that I was in the company of a lunatic.

The epigrams are never good, they never come within measurable distance of La Rochefoucauld, Balzac, or even Gohcourt. The admirers of Mr. Meredith constantly deplore their existence, admitting that they destroy all illusion of life. "When we have translated half of Mr. Meredith's utterances into possible human speech, then we can enjoy him," says the *Pall Mall Gazette*. We take our pleasures differently; mine are spontaneous, and I know nothing about translating the rank smell of a nettle into the fragrance of a rose, and then enjoying it.

Mr Meredith's conception of life is crooked, ill-balanced, and out of tune. What remains?—a certain lustiness. You have seen a big man with square shoulders and a small head, pushing about in a crowd, he shouts and works his arms, he seems to be doing a great deal, in reality he is doing nothing; so Mr. Meredith appears to me, and yet I can only think of him as an artist; his habit is not slatternly, like those of such literary hodmen as Mr. David Christie Murray, Mr. Besant, Mr. Buchanan. There is no trace of the crowd about him. I do not question his right of place, I am out of sympathy with him, that is all; and I regret that it should be so, for he is one whose love of art is pure and untainted with commercialism, and if I may praise it for nought else, I can praise it for this.

I have noticed that if I buy a book because I am advised, or because I think I ought, my reading is sure to prove sterile. *Il faut que cela vienne de moi*, as a woman once said to me, speaking of her caprices; a quotation, a chance word heard in an unexpected quarter. Mr. Hardy and Mr. Blackmore I read because I had heard that they were distinguished novelists; neither touched me, I might just as well have bought a daily paper; neither like nor dislike, a shrug of the shoulders— that is all. Hardy seems to me to bear about the same relation to George Eliot as Jules Breton does to Millet—a vulgarisation never offensive, and executed with ability. The story of an art is always the same, . . . a succession of abortive but ever strengthening efforts, a moment of supreme concentration, a succession of efforts weakening the final extinction. George Eliot gathered up all previous attempts, and created the English peasant; and following her peasants there came an endless crowd from Devon, Yorkshire, and the Midland Counties, and, as they came, they faded into the palest shadows until at last they appeared in red stockings, high heels and were lost in the chorus of opera. Mr. Hardy was the first step down. His work is what dramatic critics would call good, honest, straightforward work. It is unillumined by a ray of genius, it is slow and somewhat sodden. It reminds me of an excellent family coach—one of the old sort hung on C springs—a fat coachman on the box and a footman whose livery was made for his predecessor. In criticising Mr. Meredith I was out of sympathy with my author, ill at ease, angry, puzzled; but with Mr. Hardy I am on quite different terms, I am as familiar with him as with the old pair of trousers I put on when I sit down to write; I know all about his aims, his methods; I know what has been done in that line, and what can be done.

I have heard that Mr. Hardy is country bred, but I should not have discovered this from his writings. They read to me more like a report, yes, a report—a conscientious, well-done report, executed by a thoroughly efficient writer sent down by one of the daily papers. Nowhere do I find selection, everything is reported, dialogues and descriptions. Take for instance the long evening talk between the farm people when Oak is seeking employment. It is not the absolute and literal transcript from nature after the manner of Henri Monier; for that it is a little too diluted with Mr. Hardy's brains, the edges are a little sharpened and pointed, I can see where the author has been at work filing; on the other hand, it is not synthesized—the magical word which reveals the past, and through which we divine the future—is not seized and set triumphantly as it is in "Silas Marner." The descriptions do not flow out of and form part of the narrative, but are wedged in, and often awkwardly. We are invited to assist at a sheep-shearing scene, or at a harvest supper, because these scenes are not to be found in the works of George Eliot, because the reader is supposed to be interested in such things, because Mr. Hardy is anxious to show how jolly country he is.

Collegians, when they attempt character-drawing, create monstrosities, but a practised writer should be able to create men and women capable of moving through a certain series of situations without shocking in any violent way the most generally applicable principles of common sense. I say that a practised writer should be able to do this; that they sometimes do not is a matter which I will not now go into, suffice it for my purpose if I admit that Mr. Hardy can do this. In Farmer Oak there is nothing to object to; the conception is logical, the execution is trustworthy; he has legs, arms, and a heart; but the vital spark that should make him of our flesh and of our soul is wanting, it is dead water that the sunlight never touches. The heroine is still more dim, she is stuffy, she is like tow; the rich farmer is a figure out of any melodrama, Sergeant Troy nearly quickens to life; now and then the clouds are liquescent, but a real ray of light never falls.

The story-tellers are no doubt right when they insist on the difficulty of telling a story. A sequence of events—it does not matter how simple or how complicated—working up to a logical close, or, shall I say, a close in which there is a sense of rhythm and inevitableness is always indicative of genius. Shakespeare affords some magnificent examples, likewise Balzac, likewise George Eliot, likewise Tourgueneff; the "Œdipus" is, of course, the crowning and final achievement in the music of sequence and the massy harmonies of fate. But in contemporary English fiction I marvel, and I am repeatedly struck by the inability of writers, even of the first-class, to make an organic whole of their stories. Here, I say, the course is clear, the way is obvious, but no sooner do we enter on the last chapters than the story begins to show incipient shiftiness, and soon it doubles back and turns, growing with every turn weaker like a hare before the hounds. From a certain directness of construction, from the simple means by which Oak's ruin is accomplished in the opening chapters, I did not expect that the story would run hare-hearted in its close, but the moment Troy told his wife that he never cared for her, I suspected something was wrong; when he went down to bathe and was carried out by the current I knew the game was up, and was prepared for anything, even for the final shooting by the rich farmer, and the marriage with Oak, a conclusion which of course does not come within the range of literary criticism.

"Lorna Doone" struck me as childishly garrulous, stupidly prolix, swollen with comments not interesting in themselves and leading to nothing. Mr. Hardy possesses the power of being able to shape events; he can mould them to a certain form; that he cannot breathe into them the spirit of life I have already said, but "Lorna Doone" reminds me of a third-rate Italian opera, *La Fille du Régiment* or *Ernani*; it is corrupt with all the vices of the school, and it does not contain a single passage of real fervour or force to make us forget the inherent defects of the art of which it is a poor specimen. Wagner made the discovery, not a very wonderful one after all when we think, that an opera had much better be melody from end to end. The realistic school following on Wagner's footsteps discovered that a novel had much better be all narrative—an uninterrupted flow of narrative. Description is narrative, analysis of character is narrative, dialogue is narrative; the form is ceaselessly changing, but the melody of narration is never interrupted.

But the reading of "Lorna Doone" calls to my mind, and very vividly, an original artistic principle of which English romance writers are either strangely ignorant or neglectful, viz., that the sublimation of the *dramatis personæ* and the deeds in which they are involved must correspond, and their relationship should remain unimpaired. Turner's "Carthage" is Nature transposed and wonderfully modified. Some of the passages of light and shade—those of the balustrade—are fugues, and there his art is allied to Bach in sonority and beautiful combination. Turner knew that a branch hung across the sun looked at separately was black, but he painted it light to maintain the equipoise of atmosphere. In the novel the characters are the voice, the deeds are the orchestra. But the English novelist takes 'Any and 'Arriet, and without question allows them to achieve deeds; nor does he hesitate to pass them into the realms of the supernatural. Such violation of the first principles of narration is never to be met with in the elder writers. Achilles stands as tall as Troy, Merlin is as old and as wise as the world. Rhythm and poetical expression are essential attributes of dramatic genius, but the original sign of race and mission is an instinctive modulation of man with the deeds he attempts or achieves. The man and the deed must be cognate and equal, and the melodic balance and blending are what first separate Homer and Hugo from the fabricators of singular adventures. In Scott leather jerkins, swords, horses, mountains, and castles harmonise completely and fully with food, fighting, words, and vision of life; the chords are simple as Handel's but they are as perfect. Lytton's work, although as vulgar as Verdi's is, in much the same fashion, sustained by a natural sense of formal harmony; but all that follows is decadent,—an admixture of romance and realism, the exaggerations of Hugo and the homeliness of Trollope; a litter of ancient elements in a state of decomposition.

The spiritual analysis of Balzac equals the triumphant imagination of Shakespeare; and by different roads they reach the same height of tragic awe, but when improbability, which in these days does duty for imagination, is mixed with the familiar aspects of life, the result is inchoate and rhythmless folly, I mean the regular and inevitable alternation and combination of pa and ma, and dear Annie who lives at Clapham, with the Mountains of the Moon, and the secret of eternal life; this violation of the first principles of art—that is to say, of the rhythm of feeling and proportion, is not possible in France. I ask the reader to recall what was said on the subject of the Club, Tavern, and Villa. We have a surplus population of more than two million women, the tradition that chastity is woman's only virtue still survives, the Tavern and its adjunct Bohemianism have been suppressed, and the Villa is omnipotent and omnipresent; tennis-playing, church on Sundays, and suburban hops engender a craving for excitement for the far away, for the unknown: but the Villa with its tennis-playing, church on Sundays, and suburban hops will not surrender its own existence, it must take a part in the heroic deeds that happen in the Mountains of the Moon; it will have heroism in its own pint pot. Achilles and Merlin must be replaced by Uncle Jim and an undergraduate: and so the Villa is the only begotten of Rider Haggard, Hugh Conway, Robert Buchanan, and the author of "The House on the Marsh."

I read two books by Mr. Christie Murray, "Joseph's Coat" and "Rainbow Gold," and one by Messrs. Besant and Rice,—"The Seamy Side." It is difficult to criticise such work. It is as suited to the needs of the Villa as the baker's loaves and the butcher's rounds of beef. I do not think that any such miserable literature is found in any other country. In France some three or four men produce works of art, the rest of the fiction of the country is unknown to men of letters. But "Rainbow Gold"—to take the best of the three—is not bad as a second-rate French novel is bad; it is excellent as all that is straightforward is excellent; and it is surprising to find that work can be so good, and at the same time so devoid of artistic charm. That such a thing should be is one of the miracles of the Villa.

I have heard that Mr. Besant is an artist in the "Chaplain of the Fleet" and other novels, but this is not possible. The artist shows what he is going to do the moment he puts pen to paper, or brush to canvas; he improves on his first attempts, that is all; and I found "The Seamy Side" so very common, that I cannot believe for a moment that its author or authors could write a line that would interest me.

Mr Robert Buchanan is a type of artist that every age produces unfailingly: Catulle Mendès is his counterpart in France,—but the pallid Portuguese Jew with his Christ-like face, and his fascinating fervour is more interesting than the spectacled Scotchman. Both began with volumes of excellent but characterless verse, and loud outcries about the dignity of art, and both have—well. . . Mr Robert Buchanan has collaborated with Gus Harris, and written the programme poetry for the Vaudeville Theatre; he has written a novel, the less said about which the better—he has attacked men whose shoe-strings he is unworthy to tie, and having failed to injure them, he retracted all he said, and launched forth into slimy benedictions. He took Fielding's masterpiece, degraded it, and debased it; he wrote to the papers that Fielding was a genius in spite of his coarseness, thereby inferring that he was a much greater genius since he had sojourned in this Scotch house of literary ill-fame. Clarville, the author of "Madame Angot," transformed Madame Marneff into a virtuous woman, but he did not write to the papers to say that Balzac owed him a debt of gratitude on that account.

The star of Miss Braddon has finally set in the obscure regions of servantgalism; Ouida and Rhoda Broughton continue to rewrite the books they wrote ten years ago; Mrs. Lynn Linton I have not read. The "Story of an African Farm" was pressed upon me. I found it sincere and youthful, disjointed but well-written; descriptions of sandhills and ostriches sandwiched with doubts concerning a future state, and convictions regarding the moral and physical superiority of women: but of art nothing; that is to say, art as I understand it,—rhythmical sequence of events described with rhythmical sequence of phrase.

I read the "Story of Elizabeth" by Miss Thackeray. It came upon me with all the fresh and fair naturalness of a garden full of lilacs and blue sky, and I thought of Hardy, Blackmore, Murray, and Besant as of great warehouses where everything might be had, and even if the article required were not in stock it could be supplied in a few days at latest. These are exquisite little descriptions, full of air, colour, lightness, grace, the French life seen with such sweet English eyes, the sweet little descriptions all so gently evocative. "What a tranquil little kitchen it was, with a glimpse of the courtyard outside, and the cocks and hens, and the poplar trees waving in the sunshine, and the old woman sitting in her white cap busy at her homely work." Into many wearisome pages these simple lines have since been expanded, without affecting the beauty of the original. "Will Dampier turned his broad back and looked out of the window. There was a moment's silence. They could hear the tinkling of bells, the whistling of the sea, the voices of the men calling to each other in the port, the sunshine streamed in; Elly was standing in it, and seemed gilt with a golden background. She ought to have held a palm in her hand, poor little martyr!" There is sweet wisdom in this book, wisdom that is eternal, being simple; near may not come the ugliness of positivism, nor the horror of pessimism, nor the profound greyness of Hegelism, but merely the genial love and reverence of a beautiful-minded woman.

Such charms as these necessitate certain defects, I should say limitations. Vital creation of character is not possible to Miss Thackeray, but I do not rail against beautiful water-colour indications of balconies, vases, gardens, fields, and harvesters because they have not the fervid glow and passionate force of Titian's Ariadne; Miss Thackeray cannot give us a Maggie Tulliver, and all the many profound modulations of that Beethoven-like countryside: the pine wood and the cripple; this aunt's linen presses, and that one's economies; the boy going forth to conquer the world, the girl remaining at home to conquer herself; the mighty river holding the fate of all, playing and dallying with it for a while, and bearing it on at last to final and magnificent extinction. That sense of the inevitable which the Greek dramatists had in perfection, which George Eliot had sufficiently, that rhythmical progression of events, rhythm and inevitableness (two words for one and the same thing) is not there. Elly's golden head, the background of austere French Protestants, is sketched with a flowing water-colour brush, I do not know if it is true, but true or false in reality, it is true in art. But the jarring dissonance of her marriage is inadmissible; it cannot be led up to by any chords no matter how ingenious, the passage, the attempts from one key to the other, is impossible; the true end is the ruin, by death or lingering life, of Elly and the remorse of the mother.

One of the few writers of fiction who seems to me to possess an ear for the music of events is Miss Margaret Veley. Her first novel, "For Percival," although diffuse, although it occasionally flowed into by-channels and lingered in stagnating pools, was informed and held together, even at ends the most twisted and broken, by that sense of rhythmic progression which is so dear to me, and which was afterwards so splendidly developed in "Damocles." Pale, painted with grey and opaline tints of morning passes the grand figure of Rachel Conway, a victim chosen for her beauty, and crowned with flowers of sacrifice. She has not forgotten the face of the maniac, and it comes back to her in its awful lines and lights when she finds herself rich and loved by the man whom she loves. The catastrophe is a double one. Now she knows she is accursed, and that her duty is to trample out her love. Unborn generations cry to her. The wrath and the lamentation of the chorus of the Greek singer, the intoning voices of the next-of-kin, the pathetic responses of voices far in the depths of ante-natal night, these the modern novelist, playing on an inferior instrument, may suggest, but cannot give: but here the suggestion is so perfect that we cease to yearn for the real music, as, reading from a score, we are satisfied with the flute and bassoons that play so faultlessly in soundless dots.

There is neither hesitation nor doubt. Rachel Conway puts her dreams away, she will henceforth walk in a sad and shady path; her interests are centred in the child of the man she loves, and as she looks for a last time on the cloud of trees, glorious and waving green in the sunset that encircles her home, her sorrow swells once again to passion, and, we know, for the last time.

The mechanical construction of M. Scribe I had learnt from M. Duval; the naturalistic school had taught me to scorn tricks, and to rely on the action of the sentiments rather than on extraneous aid for the bringing about of a *dénouement*; and I thought of all this as I read "Disenchantment" by Miss Mabel Robinson, and it occurred to me that my knowledge would prove valuable when my turn came to write a novel, for the *mise en place*, the setting forth of this story, seemed to me so loose, that much of its strength had dribbled away before it had rightly begun. But the figure of the Irish politician I accept without reserve. It seems to me grand and mighty in its sorrowfulness. The tall, dark-eyed, beautiful Celt, attainted in blood and brain by generations of famine and drink, alternating with the fervid sensuousness of the girl, her Saxon sense of right alternating with the Celt's hereditary sense of revenge, his dreamy patriotism, his facile platitudes, his acceptance of literature as a sort of bread basket, his knowledge that he is not great nor strong, and can do nothing in the world but love his country; and as he passes his thirtieth year the waxing strong of the disease, nervous disease complex and torturous; to him drink is at once life and death; an article is bread, and to calm him and collect what remains of weak, scattered thought, he must drink. The woman cannot understand that caste and race separate them; and the damp air of spent desire, and the grey and falling leaves of her illusions fill her life's sky. Nor is there any hope for her until the husband unties the awful knot by suicide.

I aver that Mr. R.L. Stevenson never wrote a line that failed to delight me; but he never wrote a book. You arrive at a strangely just estimate of a writer's worth by the mere question: "What is he the author of?" for every writer whose work is destined to live is the author of one book that outshines the other, and, in popular imagination, epitomises his talent and position. Ask the same question about Milton, Fielding, Byron, Carlyle, Thackeray, Zola, Mr. Swinburne.

I think of Mr. Stevenson as a consumptive youth weaving garlands of sad flowers with pale, weak hands, or leaning to a large plate-glass window, and scratching thereon exquisite profiles with a diamond pencil. His periods are fresh and bright, rhythmical in sound, and perfect realizations of their sense; in reading you often think that never before was such definiteness united to such poetry of expression; every page and every sentence rings of its individuality. Mr. Stevenson's style is over-smart, well-dressed, shall I say, like a young man walking in the Burlington Arcade? Yes, I will say so, but, I will add, the most gentlemanly young man that ever walked in the Burlington. Mr. Stevenson is competent to understand any thought that might be presented to him, but if he were to use it, it would instantly become neat, sharp, ornamental, light, and graceful, and it would lose all its original richness and harmony. It is not Mr. Stevenson's brain that prevents him from being a thinker, but his style.

Another thing that strikes me in thinking of Stevenson (I pass over his direct indebtedness to Edgar Poe, and his constant appropriation of his methods), is the unsuitableness of the special characteristics of his talent to the age he lives in. He wastes in his limitations, and his talent is vented in prettiness of style. In speaking of Mr. Henry James, I said that, although he had conceded much to the foolish, false, and hypocritical taste of the time, the concessions he made had in little or nothing impaired his talent. The very opposite seems to me the case with Mr. Stevenson. For if any man living in this end of the century needed freedom of expression for the distinct development of his genius, that man is R.L. Stevenson. He who runs may read, and he with any knowledge of literature will, before I have written the words, have imagined Mr. Stevenson writing in the age of Elizabeth or Anne.

Turn your platitudes prettily, but write no word that could offend the chaste mind of the young girl who has spent her morning reading the Colin Campbell divorce case; so says the age we live in. The penny paper that may be bought everywhere, that is allowed to lie on every table, prints seven or eight columns of filth, for no reason except that the public likes to read filth; the poet and novelist must emasculate and destroy their work because. . . Who shall come forward and make answer? Oh, vile, filthy, and hypocritical century, I at least scorn you.

But this is not a course of literature but the story of the artistic development of me, George Moore; so I will tarry no longer with mere criticism, but go direct to the book to which I owe the last temple in my soul—"Marius the Epicurean." Well I remember when I read the opening lines, and how they came upon me sweetly as the flowing breath of a bright spring. I knew that I was awakened a fourth time, that a fourth vision of life was to be given to me. Shelley had revealed to me the unimagined skies where the spirit sings of light and grace; Gautier had shown me how extravagantly beautiful is the visible world and how divine is the rage of the flesh; and with Balzac I had descended circle by circle into the nether world of the soul, and watched its afflictions. Then there were minor awakenings. Zola had enchanted me with decoration and inebriated me with theory; Flaubert had astonished with the wonderful delicacy and subtlety of his workmanship; Goncourt's brilliant adjectival effects had captivated me for a time, but all these impulses were crumbling into dust, these aspirations were etiolated, sickly as faces grown old in gaslight.

I had not thought of the simple and unaffected joy of the heart of natural things; the colour of the open air, the many forms of the country, the birds flying,—that one making for the sea; the abandoned boat, the dwarf roses and the wild lavender; nor had I thought of the beauty of mildness in life, and how by a certain avoidance of the wilfully passionate, and the surely ugly, we may secure an aspect of temporal life which is abiding and soul-sufficing. A new dawn was in my brain, fresh and fair, full of wide temples and studious hours, and the lurking fragrance of incense; that such a vision of life was possible I had no suspicion, and it came upon me almost with the same strength, almost as intensely, as that divine song of the flesh,—Mademoiselle de Maupin.

Certainly, in my mind, these books will be always intimately associated; and when a few adventitious points of difference be forgotten, it is interesting to note how firm is the alliance, and how cognate and co-equal the sympathies on which it is based; the same glad worship of the visible world, and the same incurable belief that the beauty of material things is sufficient for all the needs of life. Mr. Pater can join hands with Gautier in saying—*je trouve la terre aussi belle que le ciel, et je pense que la correction de la forme est la vertu*. And I too join issue; I too love the great pagan world, its bloodshed, its slaves, its injustice, its loathing of all that is feeble.

But "Marius the Epicurean" was more to me than a mere emotional influence, precious and rare though that may be, for this book was the first in English prose I had come across that procured for me any genuine pleasure in the language itself, in the combination of words for silver or gold chime, and unconventional cadence, and for all those lurking half-meanings, and that evanescent suggestion, like the odour of dead roses, that words retain to the last of other times and elder usage. Until I read "Marius" the English language (English prose) was to me what French must be to the majority of English readers. I read for the sense and that was all; the language itself seemed to me coarse and plain, and awoke in me neither æsthetic emotion nor even interest. "Marius" was the stepping-stone that carried me across the channel into the genius of my own tongue. The translation was not too abrupt; I found a constant and careful invocation of meaning that was a little aside of the common comprehension, and also a sweet depravity of ear for unexpected falls of phrase, and of eye for the less observed depths of colours, which although new was a sort of sequel to the education I had chosen, and a continuance of it in a foreign, but not wholly unfamiliar medium, and so, having saturated myself with Pater, the passage to De Quincey was easy. He, too, was a Latin in manner and in temper of mind; but he was truly English, and through him I passed to the study of the Elizabethan dramatists, the real literature of my race, and washed myself clean.

XIII

Thoughts in a Strand Lodging

A wful Emma has undressed and put the last child away—stowed the last child away in some mysterious and unapproachable corner that none knows of but she; the fat landlady has ceased to loiter about my door, has ceased to tempt me with offers of brandy and water, tea and toast, the inducements that occur to her landlady's mind; the actress from the Savoy has ceased to walk up and down the street with the young man who accompanies her home from the theatre; she has ceased to linger on the doorstep talking to him, her key has grated in the lock, she has come upstairs, we have had our usual midnight conversation on the landing, she has told me her latest hopes of obtaining a part, she has told me of the husband whom she was obliged to leave; we have bidden each other goodnight; she has gone up the creaky staircase, and I have returned to my room, littered with MS. and queer publications! . . . the night is hot and heavy, but now a wind is blowing from the river, and listless and lonely I open a book, the first book that comes to hand. It is *Le Journal des Goncourts*, p. 358, the end of a chapter:—

"*It is really curious that it should be the four men the most free from all taint of handicraft and all base commercialism, the four pens the most entirely devoted to art, that were arraigned before the public prosecutor: Baudelaire, Flaubert, and ourselves.*"

Goncourt's statement is suggestive, and I leave it uncommented on; but I would put by its side another naked simple truth. That if in England the public prosecutor does not seek to over-ride literature the means of tyranny are not wanting, whether they be the tittle-tattle of the nursery or the lady's drawing-room, or the shameless combinations entered into by librarians. . . In England as in France those who loved literature the most purely, who were the least mercenary in their love, were marked out for persecution, and all three were driven into exile. Byron and Shelley, and Swinburne, he, too, who loved literature for its own sake, was forced, amid cries of indignation and horror, to withdraw his book from the reach of a public that was rooting then amid the garbage of the Yelverton divorce case. I think of these facts and think of Baudelaire's prose poem, that poem in which he tells how a dog will run away howling if you hold to him a bottle of choice scent, but if you offer him some putrid morsel picked out of some gutter hole, he will sniff round it joyfully, and will seek to lick your hand for gratitude. Baudelaire compared that dog to the public.

When I read Balzac's stories of Vautrin and Lucien de Rubempré, I often think of Hadrian and the Antinous. I wonder if Balzac thought of transposing the Roman Emperor and his favourite into modern life. It is the kind of thing that Balzac would think of. No critic has ever noticed this.

Sometimes, at night, when all is still, and I look out on that desolate river, I think I shall go mad with grief, with wild regret for my beautiful *appartement* in *Rue de la Tour des Dames*. How different the present from the past! I hate with my whole soul this London lodging, and all that concerns it—Emma, and eggs and bacon, the lascivious landlady and her lascivious daughter; I am weary of the sentimental actress who lives upstairs, I swear I will never go out to talk to her on the landing again. Then there is failure—I can do nothing, nothing; my novel I know is worthless; my life is a leaf, it will flutter out of sight. I am weary of everything, and wish I were back in Paris. I am weary of reading, there is nothing to read, Flaubert bores me. What nonsense has been talked about him! Impersonal! He is the most personal writer. But his odious pessimism! How weary I am of it, it never ceases, it is lugged in *à tout propos*, and the little lyrical phrase with which he winds up every paragraph, how boring it is. Happily, I have "A Rebours" to read, that prodigious book, that beautiful mosaic. Huysmans is quite right, ideas are well enough until you are twenty, afterwards only words are bearable. . . a new idea, what can be more insipid—fit for members of parliament. Shall I go to bed? No. I wish I had a volume of Verlaine, or something of Mallarmé's to read—Mallarmé for preference. I remember Huysmans speaks of Mallarmé in "A Rebours." In hours like these a page of Huysmans is as a dose of opium, a glass of something exquisite and spirituous.

"The decadence of a literature irreparably attacked in its organism, weakened by the age of ideas, overworn by the excess of syntax, sensible only of the curiosity which fevers sick people, but nevertheless hastening to explain everything in its decline, desirous of repairing all the omissions of its youth, to bequeath all the most subtle souvenirs of its suffering on its deathbed, is incarnate in Mallarmé in most consummate and absolute fashion. . .

"The poem in prose is the form, above all others, they prefer; handled by an alchemist of genius, it should contain in a state of meat the entire strength of the novel, the long analysis and the superfluous description of which it suppresses. . . the adjective placed in such an ingenious and definite way, that it could not be legally dispossessed of its place, would open up such perspectives, that the reader would dream for whole weeks together on its meaning at once precise and multiple, affirm the present, reconstruct the past, divine the future of the souls of the characters revealed by the light of the unique epithet. The novel thus understood, thus condensed into one or two pages, would be a communion of thought between a magical writer and an ideal reader, a spiritual collaboration by consent between ten superior persons scattered through the universe, a delectation offered to the most refined, and accessible only to them."

Huysmans goes to my soul like a gold ornament of Byzantine workmanship: there is in his style the yearning charm of arches, a sense of ritual, the passion of the Gothic, of the window. Ah! in this hour of weariness for one of Mallarmé's prose poems! Stay, I remember I have some numbers of *La Vogue*, One of the numbers contains, I know, "Forgotten Pages"; I will translate word for word, preserving the very rhythm, one or two of these miniature marvels of diction:—

I

Forgotten Pages.

"Since Maria left me to go to another star—which? Orion, Altair, or thou, green Venus?—I have always cherished solitude. What long days I have passed alone with my cat. By alone, I mean without a material being, and my cat is a mystical companion—a spirit. I can, therefore, say that I have passed whole days alone with my cat, and alone with one of the last authors of the Latin decadence; for since that white creature is no more, strangely and singularly I have loved all that the word *fall* expresses. In such wise that my favourite season of the year is the last weary days of summer, which immediately precede autumn, and the hour I choose to walk in is when the sun rests before disappearing, with rays of yellow copper on the grey walls and red copper on the tiles. In the same way the literature that my soul demands—a sad voluptuousness—is the dying poetry of the last moments of Rome, but before it has breathed at all the rejuvenating approach of the barbarians, or has begun to stammer the infantile Latin of the first Christian poetry.

"I was reading, therefore, one of those dear poems (whose paint has more charm for me than the blush of youth), had plunged one hand into the fur of the pure animal, when a barrel-organ sang languidly and melancholy beneath my window. It played in the great alley of poplars, whose leaves appear to me yellow, even in the spring-tide, since Maria passed there with the tall candles for the last time. The instrument is the saddest, yes, truly; the piano scintillates, the violin opens the torn soul to the light, but the barrel-organ, in the twilight of remembrance, made me dream despairingly. Now it murmurs an air joyously vulgar which awakens joy in the heart of the suburbs, an air old-fashioned and commonplace. Why do its flourishes go to my soul, and make me weep like a romantic ballad? I listen, imbibing it slowly, and I do not throw a penny out of the window for fear of moving from my place, and seeing that the instrument is not singing itself.

II

"The old Saxony clock, which is slow, and which strikes thirteen amid its flowers and gods, to whom did it belong? Thinkest that it came from Saxony by the mail coaches of old time?

"(Singular shadows hang about the worn-out panes.)

"And thy Venetian mirror, deep as a cold fountain in its banks of gilt work; what is reflected there? Ah! I am sure that more than one woman bathed there in her beauty's sin; and, perhaps, if I looked long enough, I should see a naked phantom.

"Wicked one, thou often sayest wicked things.

"(I see the spiders' webs above the lofty windows.)

"Our wardrobe is very old; see how the fire reddens its sad panels! the weary curtains are as old, and the tapestry on the arm-chairs stripped of paint, and the old engravings, and all these old things. Does it not seem to thee that even these blue birds are discoloured by time?

"(Dream not of the spiders' webs that tremble above the lofty windows.)

"Thou lovest all that, and that is why I live by thee. When one of my poems appeared, didst thou not desire, my sister, whose looks are full of yesterdays, the words, the grace of faded things? New objects displease thee; thee also do they frighten with their loud boldness, and thou feelest as if thou shouldst use them—a difficult thing indeed to do, for thou hast no taste for action.

"Come, close thy old German almanack that thou readest with attention, though it appeared more than a hundred years ago, and the Kings it announces are all dead, and, lying on this antique carpet, my head leaned upon thy charitable knees, on the pale robe, oh! calm child, I will speak with thee for hours; there are no fields, and the streets are empty, I will speak to thee of our furniture.

"Thou art abstracted?

"(The spiders' webs are shivering above the lofty windows.)"

We, the "ten superior persons scattered through the universe" think these prose poems the concrete essence, the osmazome of literature, the essential oil of art, others, those in the stalls, will judge them to be the aberrations of a refined mind, distorted with hatred of the commonplace; the pit will immediately declare them to be nonsense, and will return with satisfaction to the last leading article in the daily paper.

J'ai fait mes adieux à ma mère et je viens pour vous faire les miens and other absurdities by Ponson du Terrail amused us many a year in France, and in later days similar bad grammar by Georges Ohnet has not been lost upon us, but neither Ponson du Terrail nor Georges Ohnet sought literary suffrage, such a thing could not be in France, but in England, Rider Haggard, whose literary atrocities are more atrocious than his accounts of slaughter, receives the attention of leading journals and writes about the revival of Romance. As it is as difficult to write the worst as the best conceivable sentence, I take this one and place it for its greater glory in my less remarkable prose:—

"As we gazed on the beauties thus revealed by Good, a spirit of emulation filled our breasts, and we set to work to get ourselves up as well as we could."

A return to romance! a return to the animal, say I.

One thing that cannot be denied to the realists: a constant and intense desire to write well, to write artistically. When I think of what they have done in the matter of the use of words, of the myriad verbal effects they have discovered, of the thousand forms of composition they have created, how they have remodelled and refashioned the language in their untiring striving for intensity of expression for the very osmazome of art, I am lost in ultimate wonder and admiration. What Hugo did for French verse, Flaubert, Goncourt, Zola, and Huysmans have done for French prose. No more literary school than the realists has ever existed, and I do not except even the Elizabethans. And for this reason our failures are more interesting than the vulgar successes of our opponents; for when we fall into the sterile and distorted, it is through our noble and incurable hatred of the commonplace of all that is popular.

The healthy school is played out in England; all that could be said has been said; the successors of Dickens, Thackeray, and George Eliot have no ideal, and consequently no language; what can be more pudding than the language of Mr. Hardy, and he is typical of a dozen other writers, Mr. Besant, Mr. Murray, Mr. Crawford? The reason of this heaviness of thought and expression is that the avenues are closed, no new subject matter is introduced, the language of English fiction has therefore run stagnant. But if the realists should catch favour in England the English tongue may be saved from dissolution, for with the new subjects they would introduce new forms of language would arise.

"Carmen Sylva!" How easy it is to divine the æstheticism of anyone signing, "Carmen Sylva."

In youth the genius of Shelly astonished me; but now I find the stupidity of the ordinary person infinitely more surprising.

That I may die childless—that when my hour comes I may turn my face to the wall saying, I have not increased the great evil of human life—then, though I were murderer, fornicator, thief, and liar, my sins shall melt even as a cloud. But he who dies with children about him, though his life were in all else an excellent deed, shall be held accursed by the truly wise, and the stain upon him shall endure forever.

I realize that this is truth, the one truth, and the whole truth; and yet the vainest woman that ever looked in a glass never regretted her youth more than I, or felt the disgrace of middle-age more keenly. She has her portrait painted, I write these confessions; each hopes to save something of the past, and escape somehow the ravening waves of time and float into some haven of remembrance. St Augustine's Confessions are the story of a God-tortured, mine of an art-tortured, soul. Which subject is the most living? The first! for man is stupid and still loves his conscience as a child loves a toy. Now the world plays with "Robert Elsmere." This book seems to me like a suite of spacious, well distributed, and well proportioned rooms. Looking round, I say, 'tis a pity these rooms are only in plaster of Paris.

"Les Palais Nomades" is a really beautiful book, and it is free from all the faults that make an absolute and supreme enjoyment of great poetry an impossibility. For it is in the first place free from those pests and parasites of artistic work—ideas. Of all literary qualities the creation of ideas is the most fugitive. Think of the fate of an author who puts forward a new idea tomorrow in a book, in a play, in a poem. The new idea is seized upon, it becomes common property, it is dragged through newspaper articles, magazine articles, through books, it is repeated in clubs, drawing-rooms; it is bandied about the corners of streets; in a week it is wearisome, in a month it is an abomination. Who has not felt a sickening feeling come over him when he hears such phrases as "To be or not to be, that is the question?" Shakespeare was really great when he wrote "Music to hear, why hearest thou music sadly?" not when he wrote, "The apparel oft proclaims the man." Could he be freed from his ideas what a poet we should have! Therefore, let those who have taken firsts at Oxford devote their intolerable leisure to preparing an edition from which everything resembling an idea shall be excluded. We might then shut up our Marlowes and our Beaumonts and resume our reading of the bard, and the witless foists would confer happiness on many, and crown themselves with truly immortal bays. See the fellows! their fingers catch at scanty wisps of hair, the lamps are burning, the long pens are poised, and idea after idea is hurled out of existence.

Gustave Kahn took counsel of the past, and he has successfully avoided everything that even a hostile critic might be tempted to term an idea; and for this I am grateful. Nor is his volume a collection of miscellaneous verses bound together. He has chosen a certain sequence of emotions; the circumstances out of which these emotions have sprung are given in a short prose note. "Les Palais Nomades" is therefore a novel in essence; description and analysis are eliminated, and only the moments when life grows lyrical with suffering are recorded; recorded in many varying metres conforming only to the play of the emotion, for, unlike many who, having once discovered a tune, apply it promiscuously to every subject they treat, Kahn adapts his melody to the emotion he is expressing, with the same propriety and grace as Nature distributes perfume to her flowers. For an example of magical transition of tone I turn to *Intermède*.

> *"Chère apparence, viens aux couchants illuminés.*
> *Veux-tu mieux des matins albes et calmes?*
> *Les soirs et les matins ont des calmes rosâtres*
> *Les eaux ont des manteaux de cristal irisé*
> *Et des rhythmes de calmes palmes*
> *Et l'air évoque de calmes musiques de pâtres.*

* * * * *

> *Viens sous des tendelets aux fleuves souriants*
> *Aux lilas pâlis des nuits d'Orient*
> *Aux glauques étendues à falbalas d'argent*
> *A l'oasis des baisers urgents*
> *Seulement vit le voile aux seuls Orients.*

* * * * *

> *Quel que soit le spectacle et quelle que soit la rame*
> *Et quelle que soit la voix qui s'affame et brame,*
> *L'oubli du lointain des jours chatouille et serre,*
> *Le lotos de l'oubli s'est fané dans mes serres,*
> *Cependant tu m'aimais à jamais?*
> *Adieu pour jamais."*

The repetitions of Edgar Poe seem hard and mechanical after this, so exquisite and evanescent is the rhythm, and the intonations come as sweetly and suddenly as a gust of perfume; it is as the vibration of a fairy orchestra, flute and violin disappearing in a silver mist; but the clouds break, and all the enchantment of a spring garden appears in a shaft of sudden sunlight.

> *"L'éphemère idole, au frisson du printemps,*
> *Sentant des renouveaux éclorent,*
> *Se guèpa de satins si lointains et d'antan:*
> *Rose exilé des flores!*

> *Le jardin rima ses branches de lilas;*
> *Aux murs, les roses tremières;*
> *La terre étala, pour fêter les las,*
> *Des divans vert lumière;*
>
> *Des rires ailés peuplèrent le jardin;*
> *Souriants des caresses brèves,*
> *Des oiseaux joyeaux, jaunes, incarnadins*
> *Vibrèrent aux ciels de rêve."*

But to the devil with literature! Who cares if Gustave Kahn writes well or badly? I met a chappie yesterday whose views of life coincide with mine. "A ripping good dinner," he says; "get a skinful of champagne inside you, go to bed when it is light, and get up when you are rested."

Each century has its special ideal, the ideal of the nineteenth is the young man. The eighteenth century is only woman—see the tapestries, the delightful goddesses who have discarded their hoops and heels to appear in still more delightful nakedness, the noble woods, the tall castles, with the hunters looking round; no servile archæology chills the fancy; and this treatment of antiquity is the highest proof of the genius of the eighteenth century. See the Fragonards—the ladies in high-peaked bodices, their little ankles showing amid the snow of the petticoats. Up they go; you can hear their light false voices amid the summer of the leaves, where Loves are garlanded even as roses. Masks and arrows are everywhere, all the machinery of light and gracious days. In the Watteaus the note is more pensive; there is satin and sunset, plausive gestures and reluctance—false reluctance; the guitar is tinkling, and exquisite are the notes in the languid evening; and there is the Pierrot, that marvellous white animal, sensual and witty and glad, the soul of the century—ankles and epigrams everywhere, for love was not then sentimental, it was false and a little cruel; see the furniture and the polished floor, and the tapestries with whose delicate tints and decorations the high hair blends, the foot-stool and the heel and the calf of the leg that is withdrawn, showing in the shadows of the lace; see the satin of the bodices, the fan outspread, the wigs so adorably false, the knee-breeches, the buckles on the shoes, how false; adorable little comedy, adorably mendacious; and how winsome it is to feast on these sweet lies, it is indeed delight to us, wearied with the bland sincerity of newspapers. In the eighteenth century it was the man who knelt at the woman's feet, it was the man who pleaded and the woman who acceded; but in our century the place of the man is changed, it is he who holds the fan, it is he who is besought; and if one were to dream of continuing the tradition of Watteau and Fragonard in the nineteenth century, he would have to take note of and meditate deeply and profoundly on this, as he sought to formulate and synthesize the erotic spirit of our age.

The position of a young man in the nineteenth century is the most enviable that has ever fallen to the lot of any human creature. He is the rare bird, and is fêted, flattered, adored. The sweetest words are addressed to him, the most loving looks are poured upon him. The young man can do no wrong. Every house is open to him, and the best of everything is laid before him; girls dispute the right to serve him; they come to him with cake and wine, they sit circlewise and listen to him, and when one is fortunate to get him alone she will hang upon his neck, she will propose to him, and will take his refusal kindly and without resentment. They will not let him stoop to tie up his shoe lace, but will rush and simultaneously claim the right to attend on him. To represent in a novel a girl proposing marriage to a man would be deemed unnatural, but nothing is more common; there are few young men who have not received at least a dozen offers, nay, more; it is characteristic, it has become instinctive for girls to choose, and they prefer men not to make love to them; and every young man who knows his business avoids making advances, knowing well that it will only put the girl off.

In a society so constituted, what a delightful opening there is for a young man. He would have to waltz perfectly, play tennis fairly, the latest novel would suffice for literary attainments; billiards, shooting, and hunting, would not come in amiss, for he must not be considered a useless being by men; not that women are much influenced by the opinion of men in their choice of favourites, but the reflex action of the heart, although not so marked as that of the stomach, exists and must be kept in view, besides a man who would succeed with women, must succeed with men; the real Lovelace is loved by all. Like gravitation, love draws all things. Our young man would have to be five feet eleven, or six feet, broad shoulders, light brown hair, deep eyes, soft and suggestive, broad shoulders, a thin neck, long delicate hands, a high instep. His nose should be straight, his face oval and small, he must be clean about the hips, and his movements must be naturally caressing. He comes into the ball-room, his shoulders well back, he stretches his hand to the hostess, he looks at her earnestly (it is characteristic of him to think of the hostess first, he is in her house, the house is well-furnished, and is suggestive of excellent meats and wines). He can read through the slim woman whose black hair, a-glitter with diamonds, contrasts with her white satin; an old man is talking to her, she dances with him, and she refused a young man a moment before. This is a bad sign; our Lovelace knows it; there is a stout woman of thirty-five, who is looking at him, red satin bodice, doubtful taste. He looks away; a little blonde woman fixes her eyes on him, she looks as innocent as a child; instinctively our Lovelace turns to his host. "Who is that little blonde woman over there, the right hand corner?" he asks. "Ah, that is Lady—." "Will you introduce me?" "Certainly," Lovelace has made up his mind. Then there is a young oldish girl, richly dressed; "I hear her people have a nice house in a hunting country, I will dance with her, and take the mother into supper, and, if I can get a moment, will have a pleasant talk with the father in the evening."

In manner Lovelace is facile and easy; he never says no, it is always yes, ask him what you will; but he only does what he has made up his mind it is his advantage to do. Apparently he is an embodiment of all that is unselfish, for he knows that after he has helped himself, it is advisable to help someone else, and thereby make a friend who, on a future occasion, will be useful to him. Put a violinist into a room filled with violins, and he will try everyone. Lovelace will put each woman aside so quietly that she is often only half aware that she has been put aside. Her life is broken; she is content that it should be broken. The real genius for love lies not in getting into, but getting out of love.

I have noticed that there are times when every second woman likes you. Is love, then, a magnetism which we sometimes possess and exercise unconsciously, and sometimes do not possess?

XIV

Now I am full of eager impulses that mourn and howl by turns, striving for utterance like wind in turret chambers. I hate this infernal lodging. I feel like a fowl in a coop;—that landlady, those children, Emma. . . The actress will be coming upstairs presently; shall I ask her into my room? Better let things remain as they are.

Conscience.

Why intrude a new vexation on her already vexed life?

I.

Hallo, you startled me! Well, I am surprised. We have not talked together for a long time. Since when?

Conscience.

I will spare your feelings. I merely thought I would remind you that you have passed the rubicon—your thirtieth year.

I.

It is terrible to think of. My youth gone!

Conscience.

Then you are ashamed—you repent?

I.

I am ashamed of nothing—I am a writer; 'tis my profession not to be ashamed.

Conscience.

I had forgotten. So you are lost to shame?

I.

Completely. I will chat with you when you please; even now, at this hour, about all things—about any of my sins.

Conscience.

Since we lost sight of each other you have devoted your time to the gratification of your senses.

I.

Pardon me, I have devoted quite as much of my time to art.

Conscience.

You were glad, I remember, when your father died, because his death gave you unlimited facilities for moulding the partial self which the restraining influence of home had only permitted, into that complete and ideal George Moore which you had in mind. I think I quote you correctly.

I.

You don't; but never mind. Proceed.

Conscience.

Then, if you have no objection, we will examine how far you have turned your opportunities to account.

I.

You will not deny that I have educated myself and made many friends.

Conscience.

Friends! your nature is very adaptable—you interest yourself in their pursuits, and so deceive them into a false estimate of your worth. Your education—speak not of it; it is but flimsy stuff.

I.

There I join issue with you. Have I not drawn the intense ego out of the clouds of semi-consciousness, and realised it? And surely, the rescue and the individualisation of the ego is the first step.

Conscience,

To what end? You have nothing to teach, nothing to reveal. I have often thought of asking you this: since death is the only good, why do you not embrace death? Of all the world's goods it is the cheapest, and the most easily obtained.

I.

We must live since nature has willed it so. My poor conscience, are you still struggling in the fallacy of free will?

For at least a hundred thousand years man has rendered this planet abominable and ridiculous with what he is pleased to call his intelligence, without, however, having learned that his life is merely the breaking of the peace of unconsciousness, the drowsy uplifting of tired eyelids of somnolent nature. How glibly this loquacious ape chatters of his religion and his moral sense, always failing to see that both are but allurements and inveiglements! With religion he is induced to bear his misery, and his sexual appetite is preserved, ignorant, and vigorous, by means of morals. A scorpion, surrounded by a ring of fire, will sting itself to death, and man would turn upon life and deny it, if his reason were complete. Religion and morals are the poker and tongs with which nature intervenes and scatters the ring of reason.

Conscience (after a long pause).

I believe—forgive my ignorance, but I have seen so little of you this long while—that your boast is that no woman influenced, changed, or modified your views of life.

I.

None; my mind is a blank on the subject. Stay! my mother said once, when I was a boy, "You must not believe them; all their smiles and pretty ways are only put on. Women like men only for what they can get out of them." And to these simple words I attribute all the suspicion of woman's truth which hung over my youth. For years it seemed to me impossible that women could love men. Women seemed to me so beautiful and desirable—men so hideous and revolting. Could they touch us without revulsion of feeling, could they really desire us? I was absorbed in the life of woman—the mystery of petticoats, so different from the staidness of trousers! the rolls of hair entwined with so much art, and suggesting so much colour and perfume, so different from the bare crop; the unnaturalness of the waist in stays! plenitude and slenderness of silk, so different from the stupidity of a black tailcoat; rose feet passing under the triple ruches of rose, so different from the broad foot of the male. My love for the life of women was a life within my life; and oh, how strangely secluded and veiled! A world of calm colour with phantoms moving, floating past and changing in dim light—an averted face with abundant hair, the gleam of a perfect bust or the poise of a neck turning slowly round, the gaze of deep translucid eyes. I loved women too much to give myself wholly to one.

Conscience.

Yes, yes; but what real success have you had with women?

I.

Damn it! you would not seek to draw me into long-winded stories about women—how it began, how it was broken off, how it began again? I'm not Casenova. I love women as I love champagne—I drink it and enjoy it; but an exact account of every bottle drunk would prove flat narrative.

Conscience.

You have never consulted me about your champagne loves: but you have asked me if you have ever inspired a real affection, and I told you that we cannot inspire in others what does not exist in ourselves. You have never known a nice woman who would have married you?

I.

Why should I undertake to keep a woman by me for the entire space of her life, watching her grow fat, grey, wrinkled, and foolish? Think of the annoyance of perpetually looking after anyone, especially a woman! Besides, marriage is antagonistic to my ideal. You say that no ideal illumines the pessimist's life, that if you ask him why he exists, he cannot answer, and that Schopenhauer's arguments against suicide are not even plausible causistry. True, on this point his reasoning is feeble and ineffective. But we may easily confute our sensual opponents. We must say that we do not commit suicide, although we admit it is a certain anodyne to the poison of life,—an absolute erasure of the wrong inflicted on us by our parents,—because we hope by noble example and precept to induce others to refrain from love. We are the saviours of souls. Other crimes are finite; love alone is infinite. We punish a man with death for killing his fellow; but a little reflection should make the dullest understand that the crime of bringing a being into the world exceeds by a thousand, a millionfold that of putting one out of it.

Men are today as thick as flies in a confectioner's shop; in fifty years there will be less to eat, but certainly some millions more mouths. I laugh, I rub my hands! I shall be dead before the red time comes. I laugh at the religionists who say that God provides for those He brings into the world. The French Revolution will compare with the revolution that is to come, that must come, that is inevitable, as a puddle on the road-side compares with the sea. Men will hang like pears on every lamp-post, in every great quarter of London, there will be an electric guillotine that will decapitate the rich like hogs in Chicago. Christ, who with his white feet trod out the blood of the ancient world, and promised Universal Peace, shall go out in a cataclysm of blood. The neck of mankind shall be opened, and blood shall cover the face of the earth.

Conscience.

Your philosophy is on a par with your painting and your poetry; but, then, I am a conscience, and a conscience is never philosophic—you go in for "The Philosophy of the Unconscious"?

I.

No, no, 'tis but a silly vulgarisation. But Schopenhauer, oh, my Schopenhauer! Say, shall I go about preaching hatred of women? Were I to call them a short-legged race that was admitted into society only a hundred and fifty years ago?

Conscience.

You cannot speak the truth even to me; no, not even at half-past twelve at night.

I.

Surely of all hours this is the one in which it is advisable to play you false?

Conscience.

You are getting humorous.

I.

I am getting sleepy. You are a tiresome old thing, a relic of the ancient world—I mean the mediæval world. You know that I now affect antiquity?

Conscience.

You wander helplessly in the road of life until you stumble against a battery; nerved with the shock you are frantic, and rush along wildly until the current received is exhausted, and you lapse into disorganisation.

I.

If I am sensitive to and absorb the various potentialities of my age, am I not of necessity a power?

Conscience.

To be the receptacle of and the medium through which unexplained forces work, is a very petty office to fulfil. Can you think of nothing higher? Can you feel nothing original in you, a something that is cognisant of the end?

I.

You are surely not going to drop into talking to me of God?

Conscience.

You will not deny that I at least exist? I am with you now, and intensely, far more than the dear friend with whom you love to walk in the quiet evening; the women you have held to your bosom in the perfumed darkness of the chamber—

I.

Pray don't. "The perfumed darkness of the chamber" is very common. I was suckled on that kind of literature.

Conscience.

You are rotten to the root. Nothing but a very severe attack of indigestion would bring you to your senses—or a long lingering illness.

I.

'Pon my faith, you are growing melodramatic. Neither indigestion nor illness long drawn out can change me. I have torn you all to pieces long ago, and you have not now sufficient rags on your back to scare the rooks in seed-time.

Conscience.

In destroying me you have destroyed yourself.

I.

Edgar Poe, pure and simple. Don't pick holes in my originality until you have mended those in your own.

Conscience.

I was Poe's inspiration; he is eternal, being of me. But your inspiration springs from the flesh, and is therefore ephemeral even as the flesh.

I.

If you had read Schopenhauer you would know that the flesh is not ephemeral, but the eternal objectification of the will to live. Siva is represented, not only with the necklace of skulls, but with the lingam.

Conscience.

You have failed in all you have attempted, and the figure you have raised on your father's tomb is merely a sensitive and sensuous art-cultured being who lives in a dirty lodging and plays in desperate desperation his last card. You are now writing a novel. The hero is a wretched creature, something like yourself. Do you think there is a public in England for that kind of thing?

I.

Just the great Philistine that you always were! What do you mean by a "public"?

Conscience.

I have not a word to say on that account, your one virtue is sobriety.

I.

A wretched pun. . . The mass of mankind run much after the fashion of the sheep of Panurge, but there are always a few that—

Conscience.

A few that are like the Gadarene swine.

I.

Ah, . . . were I the precipice, were I the sea in which the pigs might drown!

Conscience.

The same old desire of admiration, admiration in its original sense of wonderment (miratio); you are a true child of the century; you do not desire admiration, you would avoid it, fearing it might lessen that sense which you only care to stimulate—wonderment. And persecuted by the desire to astonish, you are now exhibiting yourself in the most hideous light you can devise. The man whose biography you are writing is no better than a pimp.

I.

Then he is not like me; I have never been a pimp, and I don't think I would be if I could.

Conscience.

The whole of your moral nature is reflected in Lewis Seymore, even to the "And I don't think I would be if I could."

I.

I love the abnormal, and there is certainly something strangely grotesque in the life of a pimp. But it is nonsense to suggest that Lewis Seymore is myself; . . . you know that my original notion was to do the side of Lucien de Rubrempré that—

Conscience.

That Balzac had the genius to leave out.

I.

Really, if you can only make disagreeable remarks, I think we had better bring this conversation to a close.

Conscience.

One word more. You have failed in everything you have attempted, and you will continue to fail until you consider those moral principles—those rules of conduct which the race has built up, guided by an unerring instinct of self-preservation. Humanity defends herself against those who attempt to subvert her; and none, neither Napoleon nor the wretched scribbler such as you are, has escaped her vengeance.

I.

You would have me pull down the black flag and turn myself into an honest merchantman, with children in the hold and a wife at the helm. You would remind me that grey hairs begin to show, that health falls into rags, that high spirits split like canvas, and that in the end the bright buccaneer drifts, an old derelict, tossed by the waves of ill fortune, and buffeted by the winds into those dismal bays and dangerous offings—housekeepers, nurses, and uncomfortable chambers. Such will be my fate; and since none may avert his fate, none can do better than to run pluckily the course which he must pursue.

Conscience.

You might devise a moral ending; one that would conciliate all classes.

I.

It is easy to see that you are a nineteenth-century conscience.

Conscience.

I do not hope to find a Saint Augustine in you.

I.

An idea; one of these days I will write my confessions! Again I tell you that nothing really matters to me but art. And, knowing this, you chatter of the unwisdom of my not concluding my novel with some foolish moral. . . Nothing matters to me but art.

Conscience.

Would you seduce the wretched servant girl if by so doing you could pluck out the mystery of her being and set it down on paper?

XV

And now, hypocritical reader, I will answer the questions which have been agitating you this long while, which you have asked at every stage of this long narrative of a sinful life. [1] Shake not your head, lift not your finger, exquisitely hypocritical reader; you can deceive me in nothing. I know the base and unworthy soul. This is a magical *tête-à-tête*, such a one as will never happen in your life again; therefore I say let us put off all customary disguise, let us be frank: you have been angrily asking, exquisitely hypocritical reader, why you have been *forced* to read this record of sinful life; in your exquisite hypocrisy, you have said over and over again what good purpose can it serve for a man to tell us of his unworthiness unless, indeed, it is to show us how he may rise, as if on stepping stones of his dead self, to higher things, etc. You sighed, O hypocritical friend, and you threw the magazine on the wicker table, where such things lie, and you murmured something about leaving the world a little better than you found it, and you went down to dinner and lost consciousness of the world[2] in the animal enjoyment of your stomach. I hold out my hand to you, I embrace you, you are my brother, and I say, undeceive yourself, you will leave the world no better than you found it. The pig that is being slaughtered as I write this line will leave the world better than it found it, but you will leave only a putrid carcase fit for nothing but worms. Look back upon your life, examine it, probe it, weigh it, philosophise on it, and then say, if you dare, that it has not been a very futile and foolish affair. Soldier, robber, priest, Atheist, courtesan, virgin, I care not what you are, if you have not brought children into the world to suffer your life has been as vain and as harmless as mine has been. I hold out my hand to you, we are brothers; but in my heart of hearts I think myself a cut above you, because I do not believe in leaving the world better than I found it; and you, exquisitely hypocritical reader, think that you are a cut above me because you say you would leave the world better than you found it. The one eternal and immutable delight of life is to think, for one reason or another, that we are better than our neighbours. This is why I wrote this

---

1. The use of the word sinful here seems liable to misinterpretation. The phrase should run: "Of a virtuous life, for remember that my virtues are your vices."
2. This should run: "Forgot your hypocrisy."

book, and this is why it is affording you so much pleasure, O exquisitely hypocritical reader, my friend, my brother, because it helps you to the belief that you are not so bad after all. Now to resume.

The knell of my thirtieth year has sounded, in three or four years my youth will be as a faint haze on the sea, an illusive recollection; so now while standing on the last verge of the hill, I will look back on the valley I lingered in. Do I regret? I neither repent nor do I regret; and a fool and a weakling I should be if I did. I know the worth and the rarity of more than ten years of systematic enjoyment. Nature provided me with as perfect a digestive apparatus, mental and physical, as she ever turned out of her workshop; my stomach and brain are set in the most perfect equipoise possible to conceive, and up and down they went and still go with measured movement, absorbing and assimilating all that is poured into them without friction or stoppage. This book is a record of my mental digestions; but it would take another series of confessions to tell of the dinners I have eaten, the champagne I have drunk! and the suppers! seven dozen of oysters, pâté-de-foie-gras, heaps of truffles, salad, and then a walk home in the early morning, a few philosophical reflections suggested by the appearance of a belated street-sweeper, then sleep, quiet and gentle sleep.

I have had the rarest, the finest friends. I have loved my friends; the rarest wits of my generation were my boon companions; everything conspired to enable me to gratify my body and my brain; and do you think this would have been so if I had been a good man? If you do you are a fool, good intentions and bald greed go to the wall, but subtle selfishness with a dash of unscrupulousness pulls more plums out of life's pie than the seven deadly virtues. [3] If you are a good man you want a bad one to convert; if you are a bad man you want a bad one to go out on the spree with. And you, my dear, my exquisite reader, place your hand upon your heart, tell the truth, remember this is a magical *tête-à-tête* which will happen never again in your life, admit that you feel just a little interested in my wickedness,[4] admit that if you ever thought you would like to know me that it is because I know a good deal that you probably don't; admit that your mouth waters when you think of rich and various pleasures that fell to my share in happy Paris; admit that if this book had been an account of the pious books I had read, the churches I had been to, and the good works I had done, that

---

3. Vices, surely? See Footnote 2 above.
4. Virtue?

you would not have bought it or borrowed it. Hypocritical reader, think, had you had courage, health and money to lead a fast life, would you not have done so? You don't know, no more do I; I have done so, and I regret nothing except that some infernal farmers and miners will not pay me what they owe me and enable me to continue the life that was once mine, and of which I was so bright an ornament. How I hate this atrocious Strand lodging-house, how I long for my apartment in *Rue de la Tour des Dames*, with all its charming adjuncts, palms and pastels, my cat, my python, my friends, blond hair and dark.

The daily article soon grows monotonous, even when you know it will be printed, and this I did not know; my prose was very faulty, and my ideas were unsettled, I could not go to the tap and draw them off, the liquor was still fermenting; and partly because my articles were not very easily disposed of, and partly because I was weary of writing on different subjects, I turned my attention to short stories. I wrote a dozen. Some were printed in weekly newspapers, some were returned to me.

There was a publisher in the neighbourhood of the Strand, who used to frequent a certain bar, and this worthy man conducted his business as he dressed himself, sloppily; a dear kind soul, quite witless and quite *h*-less. From long habit he would make a feeble attempt to drive a bargain, but he was duped generally. If a fashionable author asked two hundred pounds for a book out of which he would be certain to make three, it was ten to one that he would allow the chance to drift away from him; but after having refused a dozen times the work of a Strand loafer whom he was in the habit of "treating," he would say, "Send it in, my boy, send it in, I'll see what can be done with it." There was a long counter, and the way to be published by Mr. B. was to straddle on the counter and play with a black cat. There was an Irishman behind this counter who, for three pounds a week, edited the magazine, read the MS., looked after the printer and binder, kept the accounts and entertained the visitors. I did not trouble Messrs. Macmillan and Messrs. Longman with polite requests to look at my MS., I straddled, played with the cat, joked with the Irishman, drank with Mr. B., and in the natural order of things my stories went into the magazine and were paid for. Strange were the ways of this office; Shakespeare might have sent in prose and poetry, but he would have gone into the wastepaper basket had he not previously straddled. For those who were in the "know" this was a matter of congratulation; straddling, we would cry, "We want no blooming outsiders coming along interfering with our magazine. And you, Smith, you devil, you had a twenty-page story in last month and cut me out. O'Flanagan, do you mind if I send you in a couple of poems as well as my regular stuff, that will make it all square?" "I'll try to manage it; here's the governor." And looking exactly like the unfortunate Mr. Sedley, Mr. B. used to slouch in; he would fall into his leather armchair, the one in which he wrote the cheques—the last time I saw that chair it was standing in the street in the hands of the brokers.

But conservative though we were in matters concerning "copy," though all means were taken to protect ourselves against interlopers, one who had not passed the preliminary stage of straddling would occasionally slip through our defences. One hot summer's day, we were all on the counter, our legs swinging, when an enormous young man entered. He must have been six feet three in height. He was shown into Mr. B.'s room, he asked him to read a MS., and he fled, looking very frightened. "Wastepaper basket, wastepaper basket," we shouted. "What an odd-looking fish he is—like a pike!" said O'Flanagan; "I wonder what his MS. is like." "Very like a pike," we cried. But O'Flanagan took the MS. home to read, and returned next morning convinced he had discovered an embryo Dickens. The young man was asked to call, his book was accepted, and we adjourned to the bar.

This young man took rooms in the house next to me on the ground floor. He had been to Oxford, and to Heidelberg, he drank beer and smoked long pipes, he talked of nothing but tobacco. Soon, very soon, I began to see that he thought me a simpleton; he pooh-poohed my belief in Naturalism and declined to discuss the symbolist question. He curled his long legs upon the rickety sofa and spoke of the British public as the "B.P.," and of the magazine as the "mag," and in the office which I had marked down as my own I saw him installed as a genius. He brought a little man about five feet three to live with him, and when the two, the long and the short, went out together, it was like Don Quixote and Sancho Panza setting forth in quest of adventures in the land of Strand. The short man indulged in none of the loud, rasping affectation of humour that was so maddening in the long; he was dry, hard, and sterile, and when he did join in the conversation it was like an empty nut between the teeth—dusty and bitter. He kept a pocket-book, in which he held an account of his reading. Holding the pocket-book between finger and thumb, he would say, "Last year I read ten plays by Nash, twelve by Peele, six by Greene, fifteen by Beaumont and Fletcher, and eleven anonymous plays,—fifty-four in all."

XVI

Fortunately for my life and my sanity, my interests were, about
this time, attracted into other ways—ways that led into London
life, and were suitable for me to tread. In a restaurant where low-
necked dresses and evening clothes crushed with loud exclamations,
where there was ever an odour of cigarette and brandy and soda, I
was introduced to a Jew of whom I had heard much, a man who had
newspapers and racehorses. The bright witty glances of his brown eyes
at once prejudiced me in his favour, and it was not long before I knew
that I had found another friend. His house was what was wanted, for
it was so trenchant in character, so different from all I knew of, that
I was forced to accept it, without likening it to any French memory
and thereby weakening the impression. It was a house of champagne,
late hours, and evening clothes, of literature and art, of passionate
discussions. So this house was not so alien to me as all else I had seen
in London; and perhaps the cosmopolitanism of this charming Jew, his
Hellenism, in fact, was a sort of plank whereon I might pass and enter
again into English life. I found in Curzon Street another "Nouvelle
Athènes," a Bohemianism of titles that went back to the Conquest,
a Bohemianism of the ten sovereigns always jingling in the trousers
pocket, of scrupulous cleanliness, of hansom cabs, of ladies' pet names;
of triumphant champagne, of debts, gaslight, supper-parties, morning
light, coaching; a fabulous Bohemianism; a Bohemianism of eternal
hard-upishness and eternal squandering of money,—money that rose
at no discoverable well-head and flowed into a sea of boudoirs and
restaurants, a sort of whirlpool of sovereigns in which we were caught,
and sent eddying through music halls, bright shoulders, tresses of hair,
and slang; and I joined in the adorable game of Bohemianism that was
played round and about Piccadilly Circus, with Curzon Street for a
magnificent rallying point.

After dinner a general "clear" was made in the direction of halls
and theatres, a few friends would drop in about twelve, and continue
their drinking till three or four; but Saturday night was gala night—
at half-past eleven the lords drove up in their hansoms, then a genius
or two would arrive, and supper and singing went merrily until the
chimney sweeps began to go by. Then we took chairs and bottles into
the street and entered into discussion with the policeman. Twelve hours

later we struggled out of our beds, and to the sound of church bells we commenced writing. The paper appeared on Tuesday. Our host sat in a small room off the dining-room from which he occasionally emerged to stimulate our lagging pens.

But I could not learn to see life paragraphically. I longed to give a personal shape to something, and personal shape could not be achieved in a paragraph nor in an article. True it is that I longed for art, but I longed also for fame, or was it notoriety? Both. I longed for fame, brutal and glaring.

Out with you, liars that you are, tell the truth, say you would sell the souls you don't believe in, or do believe in, for notoriety. I have known you attend funerals for the sake of seeing your miserable names in the paper! You, hypocritical reader, who are now turning up your eyes and murmuring "dreadful young man"—examine your weakly heart, and see what divides us; I am not ashamed of my appetites, I proclaim them, what is more I gratify them; you're silent, you refrain, and you dress up natural sins in hideous garments of shame, you would sell your wretched soul for what I would not give the parings of my finger-nails for— paragraphs in a society paper. I am ashamed of nothing I have done, especially my sins, and I boldly confess that I then desired notoriety.

"Am I going to fail again as I have failed before?" I asked myself. "Will my novel prove as abortive as my paintings, my poetry, my journalism?" We all want notoriety, our desire for notoriety is ugly, but it is less hideous when it is proclaimed from a brazen tongue than when it lisps the cant of humanitarianism. Self, and after self a friend; the rest may go to the devil; and be sure that when any man is more stupidly vain and outrageously egotistic than his fellows, he will hide his hideousness in humanitarianism. Victor Hugo was the innermost stench of the humanitarianism, and Mr. Swinburne holds his nose with one hand while he waves the censer with the other. Men of inferior genius, Victor Hugo and Mr. Gladstone, take refuge in humanitarianism. Humanitarianism is a pigsty, where liars, hypocrites, and the obscene in spirit congregate; it has been so since the great Jew conceived it, and it will be so till the end. Far better the blithe modern pagan in his white tie and evening clothes, and his facile philosophy. He says, "I don't care how the poor live; my only regret is that they live at all"; and he gives the beggar a shilling.

We all want notoriety; our desires on this point, as upon others, are not noble, but the human is very despicable vermin and only tolerable when it tends to the brute, and away from the evangelical. I will tell you an anecdote which is in itself an admirable illustration of my craving for notoriety; and my anecdote will serve a double purpose,—it will bring me some of the notoriety of which I am so desirous, for you, dear, exquisitely hypocritical reader, will at once cry, "Shame! Could a man be so wicked as to attempt to force on a duel, so that he might make himself known through the medium of a legal murder?" You will tell your friends of this horribly unprincipled young man, and they will, of course, instantly want to know more about him.

It was a gala night in Curzon Street, the lords were driving up in hansoms; some seated on the roofs with their legs swinging inside; the comics had arrived from the halls; there were ladies, many ladies; choruses were going merrily in the drawing-room; one man was attempting to kick the chandelier, another stood on his head on the sofa. There was a beautiful young lord there, that sort of figure that no woman can resist. There was a delightful youth who seemed inclined to empty the mustard-pot down my neck; him I could keep in order, but the beautiful lord was attempting to make a butt of me. With his impertinences I did not for a moment intend to put up; I did not know him, he was not then, as he is now, if he will allow me to say so, a friend. The ladies retired about then, and the festivities continued. We had passed through various stages of jubilation, no one was drunk, but we had been jocose and rowdy, we had told stories of all kinds. The young lord and I did not "pull well together," but nothing decidedly unpleasant occurred until someone proposed to drink to the downfall of Gladstone. The beautiful lord got on his legs and began a speech. Politically it was sound enough, but much of it was plainly intended to turn me into ridicule. I answered sharply, working gradually up crescendo, until at last, to bring matters to a head, I said,

"I don't agree with you; the Land Act of '81 was a necessity."

"Anyone who thinks so must be a fool."

"Very possibly, but I don't allow people to address such language to me, and you must be aware that to call anyone a fool, sitting with you at table in the house of a friend, is the act of a cad."

There was a lull, then a moment after he said,

"I only meant politically."

"And I only meant socially."

He advanced a step or two and struck me across the face with his finger tips; I took up a champagne bottle, and struck him across the head and shoulders. Different parties of revellers kept us apart, and we walked up and down on either side of the table swearing at each other. Although I was very wroth, I had had a certain consciousness from the first that if I played my cards well I might come very well out of the quarrel; and as I walked down the street I determined to make every effort to force on a meeting. If the quarrel had been with one of the music-hall singers I should have backed out of it, but I had everything to gain by pressing it. I grasped the situation at once. All the Liberal press would be on my side, the Conservative press would have nothing to say against me, no woman in it and a duel with a lord would be nuts and apples for the journalists.

I did not go to bed at once, but sat in the armchair thinking, calculating my chances. A cab came rattling up to the door, and one of the revellers came upstairs. He told me that everything had been arranged; I told him that I was not in the habit of allowing others to arrange my affairs for me, and went to bed.

Among my old friends I could think of some half-dozen that would suit me perfectly, but where were they? Ten years' absence scatters friends as October scatters swallows.

The first one said, "it was about one or two in the morning?"

"Later than that, it was about seven."

"He struck you, and not very hard, I should imagine; you hit him with a champagne bottle, and now you want to have him out."

"I did not come here to listen to moral reflections; if you don't like to act for me, say so."

I telegraphed to Warwickshire to an old friend:—"Can I count on you to act for me in an affair of honour?" Two or three hours after the reply came. "Come down here and stay with me for a few days, we'll talk it over." English people, I said, will have nothing to do with serious duelling. I must telegraph to Marshall. "Of all importance. Come over at once and act for me in an affair of honour. Bring the Count with you; leave him at Boulogne; he knows the colonel of the—." The next day I received the following. "Am burying my father; as soon as he is underground will come." Was there ever such ill-luck? . . . He won't be here before the end of the week. These things demand the utmost promptitude. Three or four days afterwards Emma told me a gentleman was upstairs taking a bath. "Hollo, Marshall, how are you? Had a good crossing? The poor old gentleman went off quite suddenly, I suppose?"

"Yes; found dead in his bed. He must have known he was dying, for he lay quite straight as the dead lie, his hands by his side. . . wonderful presence of mind."

"He left no money?"

"Not a penny; but I could manage it all right. Since my success at the Salon, I have been able to sell my things. I am only beginning to find out now what a success that picture was. *Je t'assure, je fais l'ècole*" . . .

"*Tu crois ça. . . on fait l'ècole après vingt ans de travail.*"

When we were excited Marshall and I always dropped into French.

"And now tell me," he said, "about this duel."

No sooner had I begun to tell the story than it dawned upon me that it was impossible to tell it seriously, for it was fundamentally an absurd story; and I lacked courage to tell Marshall that I only wished to go through with the duel in order to become notorious. No one will admit such a thing as that to his friend, and if I had admitted it Marshall would not have consented. I suddenly began to get interested in other things. There was Marshall's painting to talk about. After the theatre we went home and æstheticised till three in the morning. The duel became the least important event and Marshall's new picture the greatest. At breakfast next day the duel seemed more tiresome than ever, but the gentlemen were coming to meet Marshall. He showed his usual tact in arranging my affair of honour; a letter was drawn up in which my friend withdrew the blow of his hand, I withdrew the blow of the bottle, etc.— really now I lack energy to explain it any further.

XVII

H ypocritical reader, you draw your purity garments round you, you say, "How very base"; but I say unto you remember how often you have longed, if you are a soldier in Her Majesty's army, for war,—war that would bring every form of sorrow to a million fellow-creatures, and you longed for all this to happen, because it might bring your name into the *Gazette*. Hypocritical reader, think not too hardly of me; hypocritical reader, think what you like of me, your hypocrisy will alter nothing; in telling you of my vices I am only telling you of your own; hypocritical reader, in showing you my soul I am showing you your own; hypocritical reader, exquisitely hypocritical reader, you are my brother, I salute you.

Day passed over day, and my novel seemed an impossible task—defeat glared at me from every corner of the room. My English was so bad, so thin,—stupid colloquialisms out of joint with French idiom. I learnt unusual words and stuck them up here and there; they did not mend the style. Self-reliance had been lost in past failures; I was weighed down on every side, but I struggled to bring the book somehow to a close. Nothing mattered to me, but this one thing. To put an end to the landlady's cheating, and to bind myself to remain at home, I entered into an arrangement with her that she was to supply me with board and lodgings for three pounds a week, and henceforth resisting all Curzon Street temptations, I trudged home to eat a chop. I studied the servant as one might an insect under a microscope. "What an admirable book she would make, but what will the end be? if I only knew the end!"

I saw poor Miss L. nightly, on the stairs, and I never wearied of talking to her of her hopes and ambitions, of the young man she admired, and she used to ask me about my novel.

When my troubles lay too heavily upon me, I let her go up to her garret without a word, and remained at the window wondering if I should ever escape from Cecil Street, if I should ever be a light in that London, long, low, misshapen, that dark monumented stream flowing through the lean bridges. What if I were a light in this umber-coloured mass? Happiness abides only in the natural affections—in a home and a sweet wife. Would she whom I saw tonight marry me? How sweet she was in her simple naturalness, the joys she has known have been slight and pure, not violent and complex as mine. Ah, she is not for me, I am not fit for her, I am too sullied for her lips. Were I to win her could I be dutiful, true? . . .

XVIII

Young men, young men whom I love, dear ones who have rejoiced with me, not the least of our pleasures is the virtuous woman; after excesses there is reaction, all things are good in nature, and they are foolish young men who think that sin alone should be sought for. The feast is over for me, I have eaten and drunk; I yield my place, do you eat and drink as I have; do you be young as I was. I have written it! The word is not worth erasure, if it is not true today it will be in two years hence; farewell! I yield my place, do you be young as I was, do you love youth as I did; remember you are the most interesting beings under heaven, for you all sacrifices will be made, you will be fêted and adored upon the condition of remaining young men. The feast is over for me, I yield my place, but I will not make this leavetaking more sorrowful than it is already by afflicting you with advice and instruction how to obtain what I have obtained. I have spoken bitterly against education, I will not strive to educate you, you will educate yourselves. Dear ones, dear ones, the world is your pleasure, you can use it at your will. Dear ones, I see you all about me still, I yield my place; but one more glass I will drink with you; and while drinking I would say my last word—were it possible I would be remembered by you as a young man: but I know too well that the young never realise that the old were not born old. Farewell."

I shivered; the cold air of morning blew in my face, I closed the window, and sitting at the table, haggard and overworn, I continued my novel.

THE END

A Note About the Author

George Moore (1852–1933) was an Irish poet, novelist, memoirist, and critic. Born into a prominent Roman Catholic family near Lough Carra, County Mayo, he was raised at his ancestral home of Moore Hall. His father was an Independent MP for Mayo, a founder of the Catholic Defence Association, and a landlord with an estate surpassing fifty square kilometers. As a young man, Moore spent much of his time reading and exploring the outdoors with his brother and friends, including the young Oscar Wilde. In 1867, after several years of poor performance at St. Mary's College, a boarding school near Birmingham, Moore was expelled and sent home. Following his father's death in 1870, Moore moved to Paris to study painting but struggled to find a teacher who would accept him. He met such artists as Pissarro, Degas, Renoir, Monet, Mallarmé, and Zola, the latter of whom would form an indelible influence on Moore's adoption of literary naturalism. After publishing *The Flowers of Passion* (1877) and *Pagan Poems* (1881), poetry collections influenced by French symbolism, Moore turned to realism with his debut novel *A Modern Lover* (1883). As one of the first English language authors to write in the new French style, which openly embraced such subjects as prostitution, lesbianism, and infidelity, Moore attracted controversy from librarians, publishers, and politicians alike. As realism became mainstream, Moore was recognized as a pioneering modernist in England and Ireland, where he returned in 1901. Thereafter, he became an important figure in the Irish Literary Revival alongside such colleagues and collaborators as Edward Martyn, Lady Gregory, and W. B. Yeats.

A Note from the Publisher

Spanning many genres, from non-fiction essays to literature classics to children's books and lyric poetry, Mint Edition books showcase the master works of our time in a modern new package. The text is freshly typeset, is clean and easy to read, and features a new note about the author in each volume. Many books also include exclusive new introductory material. Every book boasts a striking new cover, which makes it as appropriate for collecting as it is for gift giving. Mint Edition books are only printed when a reader orders them, so natural resources are not wasted. We're proud that our books are never manufactured in excess and exist only in the exact quantity they need to be read and enjoyed.

Discover more of your favorite classics with Bookfinity™.

- Track your reading with custom book lists.
- Get great book recommendations for your personalized Reader Type.
- Add reviews for your favorite books.
- AND MUCH MORE!

Visit **bookfinity.com** and take the fun Reader Type quiz to get started.

Enjoy our classic and modern companion pairings!